Early Cape Breton

Early Cape Breton

is the

CJCB Radio

Book of the Year

Sponsored by CJCB Radio, the CJCB Radio Book of the Year has been established to promote good writing and publishing in Cape Breton.

Previous recipients are:

The Day the Men Went to Town
16 Stories by Women from Cape Breton

Ellison Robertson
The Last Gael
and Other Stories

Anselme Chiasson
Rosie Aucoin Grace, translator
The Seven-Headed Beast
and Other Acadian Tales
from Cape Breton Island

Sheldon Currie
The Glace Bay Miners' Museum
The Novel

EARLY
CAPE BRETON

FROM FOUNDING TO FAMINE
1784-1851

Robert Morgan

Essays, Talks, and Conversations

Breton Books

Editor: Ronald Caplan
Production Assistance: Bonnie Thompson
Photo of Cover Painting: Warren Gordon
Photo of Robert Morgan: Michael Reppa

Second printing November 2001

Our thanks to Ian MacIntosh of the McConnell Memorial Library for permission to reproduce the painting "Sydney from Hardwood Hill" by Major E. Sutherland, R.A.M.C., 1853. Our thanks, as well, to the staff of the Beaton Institute, University College of Cape Breton, for help with the illustrations. All photos courtesy the Beaton Institute. J. F. W. DesBarres's "Plan of the Town of Sydney" is courtesy Public Archives of Canada, National Map Collection.

J. F. W. DesBarres, the Founder was first published in *Nova Scotia Historical Review* (1985); **DesBarres's Plans for Sydney** in *Cape Breton's Magazine* (1985); **The Loyalists of Cape Breton**, *Dalhousie Review* (1975); **Ranna Cossit: The Loyalist Rector of St. George's Church** in *Eleven Exiles: Accounts of Loyalists of the American Revolution*, Phyllis R. Blakeley and John N. Grant eds. (1982); **Cape Breton's Debt to John Despard** in *Essays in Cape Breton History*, B. D. Tennyson ed. (1973); **"Cape Breton's Brief Time of Independence Was Over"** in *Cape Breton Post* (1985); **Separatism in Cape Breton** in *Cape Breton at 200: Historical Essays in Honour of the Island's Bicentennial 1785-1985*, Kenneth Donovan ed. (1985); **The Separatist Movement**, *Cape Breton's Magazine* (1980); **"Poverty, wretchedness, and misery," The Great Famine in Cape Breton**, *Nova Scotia Historical Review* (1986). **Governance in Cape Breton** has been published on-line by the Strategic Planning Forum on the Economy of the Cape Breton Regional Municipality at http://highlander.cbnet.ns.ca/strategy/papers.html.

THE CANADA COUNCIL | LE CONSEIL DES ARTS
FOR THE ARTS | DU CANADA
SINCE 1957 | DEPUIS 1957

We acknowledge the support of
the Canada Council for the Arts for our publishing program.

We also acknowledge support from Cultural Affairs,
Nova Scotia Department of Tourism and Culture.

Canadian Cataloguing in Publication Data

Morgan, Robert J.
  Early Cape Breton
  1st ed.
  Includes bibliographical references.
  ISBN 1-895415-60-8

1. Cape Breton Island (N.S.) — History. I. Title.

FC2343.5.M67 2000   971.6'902   C00-950144-4
F1039.C2M67 2000

CONTENTS

ILLUSTRATIONS FACING PAGES 13, 49, AND 79

1

J. F. W. DesBarres, the Founder

1784-1787

PEOPLE HAVE GREAT EXPECTATIONS of their founders: they must be brilliant, wise, saintly and preferably handsome. Various countries have insured that their national founders should fit into this mould. Hence, we have Simon Bolivar, the dashing and handsome founder of Venezuela; El Cid, the romantic leader of Spain; Augustus Caesar, founder of Imperial Rome; and, of course, George Washington who never told a lie.

Canada, unlike other countries, seems to take a delight in cutting her heroes down to size, so that they end up being anti-heroes—or worse still, clowns. Poor Sir John A. MacDonald would likely be honoured as a saint or a mighty hero, had he been a Mexican or an Italian. In Canada, there seem to be only a few statues in his honour. I remember when I was studying in Kingston, Ontario, that there was a statue of him in a park I used to pass through on my way to the university. There seemed to be a contest as to who could desecrate the statue most effectively, either by planting a gin bottle in the granite hand, or by painting the nose red. Poor MacKenzie King has suffered a similar fate at the hands of various debunkers.

In Cape Breton, we have had numerous heroes in politics, learning and labour. Perhaps fortunately, for most of them, the cold eyes of historians have not yet turned on them and they remain heroes. I am thinking of people like Angus L.

1

Macdonald, J. B. McLachlan, or even Moses Coady. We do, however, have a long-standing Cape Breton personality who is falling more and more under the microscope of history. I am speaking, of course, of Joseph Frederick Wallet DesBarres.

DesBarres has always had a special place in the hearts of Cape Bretoners. As founder of Sydney and the colony of Cape Breton, his memory has been honoured by plaques in the city and a statue raised in his honour. Dr. John Clarence Webster's 1933 biography, the *Life of Joseph Frederick Wallet DesBarres*, painted a sympathetic portrait of the man, while Will R. Bird's largely fictional *An Earl Must Have a Wife*, in 1969, portrayed our hero as a Don Juan in conflict with his mortal enemy in the Colonial Office, Lord Sydney. G. N. D. Evans, also in 1969, steered a middle, but clearly sympathetic course, in *Uncommon Obdurate: The Several Public Careers of J. F. W. DesBarres*.

It has been my task to examine DesBarres in the light of his actions as founder of Sydney and the colony of Cape Breton. Evans, who took the first serious look at DesBarres's Cape Breton career, considered him a failure. Evans, however, was dealing only with DesBarres's own brief term as lieutenant-governor of the island, and had neither the time nor the space to examine DesBarres in relation to other administrators of the early colony. How did their terms of office compare with respect to DesBarres's? Were they successes or failures? And, perhaps more importantly, just what constituted success or failure in the colony of Cape Breton?

In order to answer these questions, it is necessary to look briefly at the early history and administrative weaknesses of the island. Cape Breton was quite unlike the other Maritime colonies: in fact, it had very little going for it. When the British assumed control of the island in 1763 they refused to allow any permanent settlement during the time of Samuel Holland's survey. When Holland completed his work, his report confirmed official suspicions: the island contained rich coal resources which might attract local industry, or serve as an export to fuel industry in the Thirteen Colonies. In either case, Britain did not want competition with her own coal resources and industries; she therefore annexed the island to Nova Scotia and continued the ban on land settlement.

As a result, Cape Breton languished, while settlers were moved from New England into mainland Nova Scotia and present-day New Brunswick. With the outbreak of the American Revolution, Loyalists began pouring into the entire Maritime region except, again, Cape Breton. The population pressure, however, was mounting, and by 1784 the Colonial Office was forced to declare Cape Breton a colony open to settlement. The only difficulty was that, by this time, most of the Loyalists had already established themselves in New Brunswick and Nova Scotia. Cape Breton received no more than five hundred colonists, and the majority of these came not from New England, but from backwoods New York via Montreal and the St. Lawrence. The rest straggled in from colonies stretching from Florida to New Hampshire. The vast majority were, moreover, poor late arrivals, many of whom had failed in their first attempts at settlement elsewhere.

Another significant handicap was in the organization of the colony. Since the island had a small population of less than 2000 when the decision was made to organize it as a colony,. and since most of these were French, or illiterate English-speaking fishermen, the Colonial Office worried that the infant colony would not be able to survive by itself or support a house of assembly. As a result, it was made an adjunct colony of Nova Scotia and, although granted a representative assembly, that body was not to be called until the population of the island warranted it.[1] In theory, the lieutenant-governor of Cape Breton was subordinate to the lieutenant-governor of Nova Scotia. Should the lieutenant-governor of the latter be physically present in Cape Breton, he could assume control of the island's government. In reality this never happened, but it did give the lieutenant-governor of Nova Scotia leave to interfere in and report to the Colonial Office on events in Cape Breton. This, in turn, seriously weakened the power of the island government.

The purpose behind making Cape Breton an adjunct colony may have been to compensate for the delayed house of assembly since, with no elected body to act as a brake on the appointed council, there might be a danger of executive dictatorship. In effect, quite the opposite happened. The Executive Council became, instead, a battleground of factions contending for power. Since there was no elected house of assembly where debate would normally occur, the Executive Council filled that job. This tended to stymie the work of the Council, and furthermore, to pull the various lieutenant-governors into the ongoing fights of the council members.

When the lieutenant-governors took sides, as they all eventually did, the opposing group had two options: resign, or complain to outside sources. The opposition generally chose the latter, approaching the lieutenant-governor of Nova Scotia, asking him to obtain redress on their behalf from the Colonial Office. If the lieutenant-governor of Nova Scotia was convinced of their arguments, or felt any enmity toward the lieutenant-governor of Cape Breton, the former's interference might indeed help precipitate the latter's dismissal. The power of the lieutenant-governor in Cape Breton was thus considerably weakened.

There was another outstanding weakness in the colony's organization. Since Cape Breton had no house of assembly, taxes could not be collected. Without taxes, public improvements could not be made. Roads, bridges and public buildings were therefore bound to be neglected, which in turn held back settlement and was a source of frustration to administrators.

The economic development of the colony was further retarded by a lack of capital. The chief taxable resource of the island was the government-owned coalfields, but Great Britain could hardly be expected to invest money in a resource which might compete with her own assets. As a result, the coal mines were not developed efficiently. Scarce private capital was pressed into service when possible, but it was always too little.

In any case, one could hardly expect private capital to invest in government-owned coalfields whose markets, due to the Navigation Laws, were restricted, in effect, to Halifax, still a small town.[2] Even there, coal could be imported more cheaply from Britain than from Cape Breton. Consequently, the colonial government usually operated the mines, while the shipping fees and small profits occurring from the export venture were used to develop the coalfields and to help with public improvements. The only other sources of income for the colony were the salaries paid to officials, plus a small contingency allowance of between £500 and £1,000, voted annually by Parliament.

Let us recall that Cape Breton was organized as a separate colony because of a need to settle Loyalists. The same, of course, held true for New Brunswick, but the latter differed from Cape Breton in that when the decision to organize into a separate colony was made, New Brunswick already had some 20,000 to 30,000 settlers in place. There was no doubt that they would demand and receive a house of assembly, which would permit taxation and local improvement. Even Prince Edward Island, with a smaller population but powerful allies in London, received a representative assembly. Cape Breton had neither the population nor the allies to protect her interests.

Yet a government was set up in Cape Breton, and Loyalists came looking for land, government jobs and largesse to compensate for their considerable losses in the Thirteen Colonies after the American War of Independence. Refugees like Abraham Cuyler, former mayor of Albany, New York, and

David Mathews, former mayor of New York City, to name only two of the most influential, considered power and remuneration their right when they arrived in Cape Breton. Although only a small number of Loyalists came, there were too many of them seeking too few jobs for themselves and their friends, complaining in frustration to Halifax and London, and threatening to grind the poor Cape Breton colony's development to a halt.

Any lieutenant-governor or administrator involved in this situation was entering a minefield laid with booby traps at every step. Of the ten lieutenant-governors or administrators between 1785 and 1820, four were dismissed, two resigned, one served eight months, another only two and one half years. The last lieutenant-governor, George Robert Ainslie, was asking for a transfer when the colony of Cape Breton was re-annexed to Nova Scotia. Lieutenant-Governor William Macarmick survived the longest—eight years—using his government connections, and those of his aristocratic wife, to shelter him from the attacks of his enemies in Sydney and Halifax.

IT IS AGAINST THIS BACKGROUND that we must assess the career of J. F. W. DesBarres in Cape Breton. Since he was the founder and first lieutenant-governor of the colony, his successors, forewarned of the problems inherent in the local organizations had, perhaps, an advantage over him. On the other hand, his attitudes only worsened the situation.

Briefly, when the Colonial Office decided to set up the colony of Cape Breton, DesBarres was considered as lieutenant-governor because of his knowledge of the place: he had served at the fall of Louisbourg, and had just completed a coastal survey of Cape Breton and Nova Scotia which had been published as the *Atlantic Neptune*. More importantly, since the Admiralty—for whom DesBarres had produced the charts—was slow in remunerating him, the appointment may be seen as compensation, rather than reward for true administrative abilities.

Apart from this, DesBarres, who was convinced of the great importance of the Maritimes in general, was particularly enthusiastic about the new colony's potential as a Loyalist refuge and as a fishing and mining area. He felt that the revenue resulting from these resources could easily cover the costs of governing and developing the island,[3] but failed to take into account the strangling effect of the Navigation Laws, as well as the plans to defer an elected assembly in Cape Breton.

The British government was culpable in both its slow payment for the *Atlantic Neptune* and its failure to provide sufficient stimulus to the development of the Cape Breton economy. However, DesBarres's personality exacerbated the situation and imperiled the colony even further. DesBarres was a man of vision, one who was able to see the potential of any person or situation. As such, he was single-minded and pursued his vision in the most direct way possible. This often meant brushing aside institutions, bureaucracies and people's feelings, in the pursuit of his goal. Like a terrier, he ferreted out his object and hung on till he achieved success.

In the case of the *Atlantic Neptune*, for example, he worked like a man possessed, with a staff of usually seven assistants and from twenty to thirty labourers. He pushed himself and his men to the limit, through uncharted and dangerous waters—and almost drowned on Sable Island—all because he was determined to complete an accurate survey of the coasts and harbours of Nova Scotia. When his superiors noticed the bills piling up and tried to limit the survey to the Atlantic coasts alone, DesBarres fought and won permission to complete not only the entire Nova Scotian and Cape Breton shorelines, but also the coast down to New York. The final expenses, as we have seen, resulted in late payment for the *Neptune*, and even when DesBarres's demands for complete compensation were eventually fulfilled in 1794, he was never happy with the settlement. A less single-minded person would have followed the line of least resistance, produced the charts, and received payment, with much less furor.

We see similarities in DesBarres's behaviour in Cape Breton. It has already been noted that the economic potential of the island was handicapped by a faulty constitution and the Navigation Laws. On the other hand, the new lieutenant-governor saw only the great potential of his colony "to be considered by the rivals of our country [*sic*] with an envious eye"[4] and was determined to be the prime instrument to this end. He acted as if his Executive Council and the Navigation Laws did not exist.

In order to get buildings erected and streets cleared in Sydney as quickly as possible, [in 1785-86] DesBarres issued supplies as payment to both Loyalists and non-Loyalists alike. There was doubt whether non-Loyalists were entitled to this bounty, but even worse, he did this without government permission.[5] Worse still, he did not consult the Loyalist members of his Executive Council, like Cuyler and Mathews. The latter, seeing their power slipping, complained to the commander of the garrison, Lieutenant-Colonel John Yorke, who insisted that, *ex officio*, he too had a right to issue supplies. According to instructions, supplies were to be issued by the local troop commander, but DesBarres, as lieutenant-governor, was described as "commanding his Majesty's Forces in Cape Breton and its Dependencies," and he was not about to allow the military to interfere with his civil authority.[6] The colony was divided between those supporting DesBarres and those supporting Cuyler, Mathews and Yorke.

Meanwhile, the supplies were being depleted and there was danger of starvation during the coming winter. Since Britain had failed to send adequate provisions to Halifax, the hope of assistance from that quarter was growing dimmer.[7] Yorke finally agreed to a compromise, but DesBarres refused unless Yorke gave him complete control over supplies. The lieutenant-governor even went so far as to buy supplies on his own account, for which he did not obtain final compensation until 1802. In the end, the town averted starvation when Des-Barres, hearing of a shipwreck off Arichat, sent a party there to seize supplies found aboard the ship. However, the damage had been done and the colony's chief Loyalists were soon writing to Lieutenant-Governor John Parr of Nova Scotia, who quickly conveyed their complaints to Lord Sydney.

Still another incident reveals DesBarres's impetuousness and consequent determination to act on his own. Obviously disappointed that so few Loyalists had come and stayed in Cape Breton, he decided to recruit new settlers. Like Holland, he realized the potential value of the fishery, and on his own, he therefore decided to send a Cape Breton merchant, Captain Thomas Venture, to Nantucket with a proclamation promising land and good anchorage to whalers who were thinking of moving to British territory. The difficulty was that both Halifax—and more importantly, the British—wanted whalers to settle in their jurisdictions. DesBarres typically ignored this and informed the Colonial Office of his intentions only after he had sent Venture on his journey. Of course, he not only failed to acquire the whalers, but also received a black mark from Lord Sydney for his independent and impudent actions.[8]

The very characteristics of imagination, courage and independent action that spelt success for the *Atlantic Neptune* led to DesBarres's failures as a lieutenant-governor. In the light of his successors' careers, however, DesBarres did not fare badly. As already noted, the British government's colonial policy, the organization of the colony itself, and the power-hungry Cape Breton Loyalists all conspired to cripple later governors as well.

For all his failures, moreover, DesBarres had various successes in his colony. Having chosen a site for his capital, he planned it with great foresight; one town planner has called Sydney "the only imaginatively planned project in 18th century Nova Scotia."[9] By the end of the first year of the colony's existence, DesBarres could boast that he and his little band of no more than two hundred settlers had erected a barracks, hospital, mess house, carpenter's shop, governor's quarters, bakehouse, provision store, jail, and teacher's house in Sydney. He had also attracted the colony's first minister, Ranna Cossit, who eventually began the first church and school in English Cape Breton.

The coal mines were a great challenge, since the British government, as we have noted, was totally uninterested in their development. As proof, DesBarres was given no instructions concerning them; accordingly, he ran them on his own account and hired a collier, Thomas Moxley. With no capital, Moxley simply dug pits to remove surface coal, and actually damaged the coal seams. DesBarres made very little money from the venture and, indeed, he tackled the project more in hopes of attracting interest and revenue to the colony than in anticipation of personal gain.

This is not to say that DesBarres did not stand to prosper from the development of Cape Breton; like other governors, he expected to make a profit from his appointment. His particular interest, however, was land speculation and management in mainland Nova Scotia and New Brunswick. In Cape Breton, he confined himself to a large tract of land in Point Edward, which he wanted to develop as a model farm for future profit. It was therefore in his own self-interest that the colony he founded should prosper. In reality, he eventually sold the model farm and made very little money from it.

Before we make our final assessment of DesBarres as lieutenant-governor of Cape Breton and founder of Sydney, we must quickly place the colony in context. DesBarres may have seen Cape Breton as the hope of the British Empire but the Colonial Office was hardly aware of its existence. Neither the island's fish, coal, nor timber were of any importance to the Mother Country. The colony was only convenient as a place to deposit Loyalists clamouring for office. Only the smallest amounts of money were ever spent there, and when Cape Breton was re-annexed to Nova Scotia in 1820, the island's roads, public buildings and facilities were so far behind those of the mainland that it took almost half a century to overcome the neglect. All Britain asked was that the colony exist quietly and ask for nothing. However, by granting her an absurd constitution and appointing as lieutenant-governor a man of DesBarres's vitality, the Colonial Office received a rude awakening.

In the end, DesBarres was dismissed because he disturbed the peace of Whitehall [London]. Formally he was accused of causing friction between Cape Breton and Nova Scotia and between the civil and military authorities on the island, and of wasting money by distributing supplies to people unentitled to them.[10] It is poetic justice that his dismissal did not result in a subdued Cape Breton, but served instead as a prelude to continued unrest in the disadvantaged colony.

When we examine all these factors, we cannot claim that DesBarres was either a magnificent hero or an utter failure in Cape Breton. He faced the problems we still face today: restrictive trade policies, distance from markets, a low priority in the development schemes of government, rivalry with a more powerful Halifax, and the internal squabbling of too many people seeking too few jobs. He tried to deal with these problems directly, but treaded on too many toes. The vision that led to the masterpiece of the *Atlantic Neptune* resulted ultimately in his downfall as an administrator in Cape Breton.

Two portraits of J.F.W. DesBarres, founder of the Cape Breton colony; a painting, "Founding of Sydney, 1785," by Lieut. Booth, August 1785; and a photo of the Old Barracks at Victoria Park. *Courtesy the Beaton Institute, University College of Cape Breton.*

2

DesBarres's Plans for Sydney

A CONVERSATION

DESBARRES IS KIND OF a mysterious eighteenth-century character—and he always kept himself purposely mysterious. I think this is one of the interesting essences of his character that you can't put in a biography.

DesBarres was purposely fuzzy about his background, his family, his relationships, even the number of children he had. To capture the man in print is very difficult, because your documents don't tell you. I don't care if you talk about where he was born, his education, how he got to Cape Breton, what he did when he got here, why he did what he did in Cape Breton, about the *Atlantic Neptune*, about his later years in Halifax, his relationship with his mistress Mary Cannon, the way he managed his estates in Nova Scotia and New Brunswick mainland—all of these things—there's always something mysterious, there's always something missing, there's always something that you come against. And I think that's the first statement you have to make about DesBarres, is that he, I think purposely, did this.

I mean, was he born in France or Switzerland? We're not even sure. When did he come to Britain? Well, we're not too sure.

You could say he did that because England and France were frequently at war. He'd be careful about saying where he came from, because he wanted to get ahead. A very ambitious man, that's for sure. So perhaps that's why he's purposefully being vague.

And it goes all the way through like that. Like when he does the *Atlantic Neptune*, which is the great hydrographic survey of the coasts of eastern North America. Which is the first really detailed investigation of the coasts—measuring the coastline and, more important, the depths of water. It's hard to believe, but before that time, nobody had clear ideas of the depths of the water all along that coast. And with the approach of the American Revolution, the British could see if they were going to maintain the colonies along the coast, they were going to have to beef up their fleet and they were going to have to be very certain as to where their ships could and could not go.

DesBarres had had a lot of experience before this. For example, he had been present at the siege of Louisbourg back in 1759, and he'd surveyed the harbour at Louisbourg after the fall [of the fortress]. And he'd also done work in harbours in Newfoundland, and Halifax Harbour—surveyed the harbour with a view to perfecting the defenses there. He was also present at the siege of Quebec. And he'd done work with Captain Cook when Cook was just beginning. Cook had surveyed the whole St. Lawrence River. DesBarres had had training at the Royal Military Academy at Woolich, at Greenwich, England, which is the great naval base. In other words, he had had experience and training in surveying, in hydrography, and engineering.

So he was a good choice. He put his name forward. He was never shy about putting his name forward. Some of the others were.

For example, Captain Samuel Holland, who surveyed Cape Breton just previous to this, was a little bit shyer person. DesBarres was always very outgoing, and always pushy. He was always writing petitions asking for jobs. I don't know where he got the time. You'd have to live to be 103 or 104 just to have the time. [Recent research has called even his age into doubt, suggesting that DesBarres lived to be about 93.] I think he spent at least ten years of that just sitting down writing.

Anyway, he got the job, and he did the surveys. He was given a crew and a couple of ships. But he literally, literally, did the work. He went out in boats for weeks, months, at a time. And they'd work all summer. And in the winter, they would pull them together, draw maps of the coastline, which were later published as the *Atlantic Neptune*. There's charts, from above, which give the depths, like a regular map. And then, there are some that he did as views—how it would appear from the sea. So you might see a view of Sydney Harbour, let's say, which can be very strange looking at it from the sea— it's just two little humps and the entrance, you know, Cranberry on one side and Low Point on the other. What to look for [a guide for coming safely into the harbour]. There's a sandbar here—so there might be a chart from above, showing the depths and the sandbars and the difficulties. And it's hard to believe this hadn't been done much before. And it's DesBarres who did this. So this is an enduring monument.

They would do the surveys. And then in the winter, they'd go to a place he'd purchased in the Falmouth area of Nova Scotia. A large estate, he'd built this huge mansion which he called Castle Frederick, with which the people up around Windsor are familiar. And that's where he would spend his winters, putting the maps together, drawing them up, and preparing them for the Admiralty. And when this was done, they were sent over to England for publication.

The difficulty is that he kept taking some maps out and putting new maps in, changing it. So you can't point to anywhere and say, "This is the complete *Atlantic Neptune*." The *Atlantic Neptune*—typical DesBarres. There was no one copy that you can say is the final version of *Atlantic Neptune*. It's sort of like quicksilver, and an awful lot like him.

So he was working on this all through the 1770s and early '80s. And, typical of the bureaucracy, money was always late coming in. Policies of the government would change, and they lost interest in it. Then they got very interested when the American Revolution broke out, extremely interested in charts he'd done. As the Revolution went on, well, they weren't so interested any more. But of course DesBarres, being the type he was, he was determined he was going to finish this. He was out of pocket quite often—paying his surveyors, the money was late coming across the ocean.

So the government owed him money—always seemed to owe DesBarres. And there was always controversy over his accounts, which were never accurate. Now, I don't know if that was on purpose, or if it was just the way he was, or if it was because the Colonial Office was always in such a mess. And that's something we often forget. The government didn't have enough clerks, their records weren't good. The government would lose accounts! Extremely inefficient. But they always owed him.

So he was under pressure. Artistic man, under pressure. Very, very desirous of getting ahead. And he had a wife in England, and a number of children. And this is when he takes up with Mary Cannon, a lady in Nova Scotia. She becomes his mistress. He has a number of children from her.

He was fond of these children, as he was of his own. But you've got to remember eighteenth-century attitudes towards sex, towards marriage, are in many ways different from now, I suspect. He seemed to find no problem with maintaining two households. He never shows any qualms of conscience. And it's almost as if he had a family in Nova Scotia and he had a family in England. But his first loyalty was to his own, his natural offspring, and to his wife. When he left his estates—he acquired numerous ones, in Cumberland County in particular, and later in Cape Breton—Mary Cannon runs these estates while he's away. He goes to England for a number of years to peddle the *Atlantic Neptune* and for legal purposes, to get the money that's owed him—and Mary Cannon ran the estates.

And she writes to him continually, asking him, "What do I do in this situation?" You know, trying to get the rents from the people. And he gave her no help at all. But she felt she had power of attorney, to sell land and make exchanges and things like this. And he later disavowed all this of her, in what we would consider a very heartless manner. There's no doubt that in that case he was a scoundrel.

But again, it's hard to know what his attitude toward Mary Cannon was, and what he felt about her. Whether he saw this as a business deal, totally a business deal, or simply had so much else on his mind when he was in England—and he did have a lot on his mind—that he just washed his hands of this. Maybe he wanted to escape from it. He's a mysterious man, as I say. He never strikes me particularly as an escapist when he comes here to Cape Breton, or later in Prince Edward Island. But I think that, emotionally, he may have been an escapist.

(Interviewer: *We have no evidence of this?*) No, that's right, I'm just talking to this. All we have are letters back and forth, or no letters back and forth, which is even worse. Him not answering Mary Cannon's letters when she's begging for help. And then suddenly cutting her off and throwing her out. Maybe he saw it as self-preservation. Living in a world where it's sink or swim. And it was bad then—a foreigner—and his accounts were called into question, his honesty was called into question. He had no money to speak of. He could have been destroyed by the government. His whole life was spent fighting for what he thought was right for himself, to keep himself above water. He's always fighting.

You know, he's a complicated person. He's not a simple person. And the problem is—his papers are great, we have huge amounts of papers, but he doesn't come across. Again, he may have destroyed them—he was very careful about it. (*If they ever existed.*) If they were ever there.

(*So he has moved on to a new phase of his life, the post-*Atlantic Neptune.) Exactly. And that next phase centres around a number of things. By 1783 he publishes the *Atlantic Neptune*. And at the same year, the American Revolution is over. And the Americans get their independence. And the Admiralty still owes DesBarres money for the *Atlantic Neptune*. And he is going to get that money. No one is going to prevent him from getting his due. That's when Cape Breton comes into the scene.

Loyalists are moving up from the United States. And the Colonial Office hits upon the idea—having been coaxed into it by Abraham Cuyler, the former mayor of Albany, New York, with a band of Loyalists—to make Cape Breton a separate colony. Samuel Holland, in his survey of the coast of North America in 1763, had suggested that Cape Breton would make a good separate province. Now the British government looked at this as a place to put Loyalists. Because Quebec was rapidly filling, and they didn't want any trouble, with too many Englishmen in a French area. And they were moving into Ontario, of course. But that was still utter *terra incognito*.

But there was this nice little place here, on the coast. The only problem was that Britain didn't want to spend any money. But Holland had pointed out that, going back to the days of Louisbourg, less than thirty years previously, there was prosperity here, a very booming French colony. Plus, Holland had pointed out, and DesBarres had seen, the coal reserves. So the idea was that this place had a great potential for lumbering, agriculture, fishing, of course, and coal mining.

The Colonial Office, sometime in the summer of 1784, had come to the conclusion that they were going to break Cape Breton away from Nova Scotia. So who was going to be the governor? DesBarres was in London by that time, trying to get his payment for the *Atlantic Neptune*. And he felt that he would be an obvious choice.

Meanwhile, Abraham Cuyler had got wind of this [the decision to make Cape Breton a separate colony]. Cuyler had hightailed it over to England at the same time, in early 1784, to the Colonial Office, to say, "I can bring 3000 Loyalists to Cape Breton." And he had ambitions to be, if not governor, at least in the government of the new colony. Now, there's no record of DesBarres's having met Cuyler there during this time. Both ambitious men. Both looking to run the colony. And that was never resolved, really. Even after the colony began, DesBarres and Cuyler fought; they never got along. And Cuyler was finally part of the downfall of DesBarres as governor of Cape Breton colony.

At any rate, DesBarres pushed his case with numerous requests, numerous petitions, I mean 25-, 30-page petitions, in which he lays out his whole career. He sends these petitions to Lord North and, later, Lord Sydney. And convinces them that the colony can be run efficiently.

Now remember, Britain has just fought a war, so she's broke. She's got to pay all these Loyalists who, because they've been loyal, have lost property in the States and are asking compensation from the British government. And Britain has to recompense them for their loyalty. And Britain had fought the Seven Years War with France, and then she had fought the American war, and she's fighting in India. There'd been a great drain on the treasury. So DesBarres uses this and says, "Look, the colony can run on its own. And you owe me money. So why not appoint me governor, and we'll call it even?"

So the deal is struck on that ground. The Colonial Office decides on that way to get out of the money they owe him. Plus, they pay off a whole crowd of other Loyalists. (*Paid them off in what form?*) Land grants here in Cape Breton. Two hundred acres free. Plus—in the case of Cuyler—by giving him office, making him secretary of the colony. There's a regular pay, a good pay.

New Brunswick was in the same situation, and was set off at the same time. But New Brunswick was different, because something like 20,000 or 30,000 people had poured in there between 1780 and 1783. They were there already when they were proclaimed a colony in 1784. Cape Breton in 1784— there was nobody to speak of here. I mean, there were a few people living in Louisbourg, fishermen, and some Acadians down around Arichat. Mi'kmaq, of course. You might as well say Cape Breton was empty. Just a small population of probably no more than 2000 people. And the colony wasn't declared for these people, anyway. It was declared to pay off debts to the Loyalists.

DesBarres is in England. He doesn't get to Cape Breton until January of 1785. His first task is to get a ship and to get a number of settlers. He wants to get craftsmen, carpenters and masons—this sort of thing. He gets about 120 settlers, through the fall. (*These are not Loyalists?*) No, these are the Muggahs and the Rudderhams and these people, who make up an important part of the population of Sydney now. They're simply Englishmen, from the West Country mainly. Because DesBarres doesn't know what he's got among this Loyalist mob that's coming up.

When Cuyler found out that Cape Breton was going to be a separate colony, he immediately sent back word on the next ship across to tell his people—they were in Quebec City, these Loyalists—to set sail for Cape Breton. And they did. But instead of 3000, there was only something like a couple of hundred. They'd gotten frightened. Before word got through that yes, you can go to Cape Breton—a lot of them went to Upper Canada.

Cuyler's people came in three ships, the *Liberty*, the *Sally*, and the *Saint Peter*. Two of the ships landed at St. Peters, and one went on to Louisbourg. And no thought of going to Sydney Harbour. Does that mean that DesBarres didn't talk to Cuyler? Or does it mean that DesBarres wasn't sure Sydney was going to be the capital? Or he hadn't told Cuyler his plans to make Sydney the capital, not wanting Cuyler to get there before he arrived? We don't know. It's not documented.

So Cuyler's people came. And Cuyler came across the ocean and joined them at Louisbourg. By August 1784 they're there. The people in St. Peters winter. And the following spring they go to Baddeck. My guess is the majority went to Baddeck, and left their wives and children back at Louisbourg or St. Peters, until they could get themselves established. Jonathan Jones had already reconnoitered the Baddeck area. While Cuyler had gone to England, Jonathan Jones had sailed up, at Cuyler's request, to find a good place to settle. And Jones hit upon what we call Big Baddeck, back up the Baddeck River—that's where the original Baddeck was. Little Baddeck [the village today] is later. And when they got their farms settled up, then the wives and children joined them.

Meanwhile, DesBarres is organizing his ship, the *Blenheim*. And it comes across with supplies and tools and people—120. Without DesBarres, though. We have no record of Cuyler having supplies. So the *Blenheim* goes across. And it's interesting. Instead of going right to Sydney Harbour, it goes to Louisbourg. Sees Cuyler's people there, and sees they're in very bad condition. And a lot fewer than he expected. And DesBarres's not there; let's say just the captain of the *Blenheim* sees this. DesBarres's still in England. Louisbourg's a terrible situation. There's only four houses left standing that are habitable. No supplies. Cuyler's people are just about half dead.

Now, we don't know whether DesBarres had said [to his people], "Go to Louisbourg, see if there's a crowd; and if there's good supplies, we'll go there. If things aren't so good, go to Spanish Bay [present Sydney Harbour]." Because Samuel Holland had previously said, "Spanish Bay is the place. There's no fog, and it's free from all the problems of Louisbourg." And he had thought Point Edward—as he called it, Edwardstown—would be the perfect place to settle. In any case, that's just what these people do. So I presume that Samuel Holland must have had some kind of influence on DesBarres. DesBarres, when he did the *Atlantic Neptune* survey, had had Holland's plans and had made a special little trip to Sydney, to Spanish Bay.

They go around Point Edward, and they arrive in November. And it's a snowstorm. The *Blenheim* is being tossed around. They decide to unload their supplies. Whether it's the tip of Point Edward, or Crawley's Creek, we'll never know. And at the Mines, there are some buildings still standing. The British troops had been mining there until 1784. So there were barracks. They decided to house the people there for the winter. And that's good, to keep people away from the supplies. (*And close to the coal.*) Well, exactly. And that's an important point. They're near the source of fuel. And it's sort of symbolic as the coal was going to be very important in this new colonial setup.

Meanwhile, DesBarres leaves England, sails across the ocean to Halifax, where he sees the governor of Nova Scotia. He received his orders—this is all formal—and then came to Cape Breton. He arrived in January on the coast. He would meet Cuyler and his people, who were still down in Louisbourg. You've got the *Blenheim* people living in Spanish Bay, and you've got Cuyler's people down at Louisbourg. They remained separate. And DesBarres sees them, and then he finds out where his people are. (*And sees Cuyler's situation.*) Oh yes—terrible, wretched. We don't know what the conversation was, or what transpired. All we know is that DesBarres takes a sleigh across and comes here, to Spanish Bay. And during that winter, Cuyler and his people come up here. They realize that the capital's not going to be Louisbourg.

In February he has his first meeting of the colonial Council at the Mines. You could date the beginning of the Cape Breton colony with the first meeting of the Council. This is how I see the founding of the colony. He stepped ashore at Louisbourg, but my feeling of sort of this beginning of the colony, in reality, is February 15th, 1985—when the first Council meeting is called, and he's proclaimed governor in a formal manner, and they have their first minutes. (*And this all takes place in what we call Sydney Mines?*) Yes. And I am sure people in Sydney Mines don't realize this. It started there.

(*And this is just as fuzzy as DesBarres himself. You don't know exactly when Cape Breton colony gets formed, or declared.*) Well, when is a colony declared? Is it declared when Britain makes the big statement, or is it declared when the first settlers come, or is it declared when the lieutenant-governor comes? We had this problem when we were going to mark the bicentennial. (*If he'd come ashore and planted the cross!*) If he'd done that, that'd be lovely—we'd know. But that just didn't happen. We had this debate about the bicentennial—when are we going to celebrate it? Well, we're not celebrating Britain declaring this a separate colony, in 1784. There were no people here. And we're not celebrating the fact that Britain did this. We're not rejoicing in our Britishness. We're celebrating the founding of our colony, of our people coming here. If that's the case, it's sometime in 1785, when the Council began, and the people's representation began.

So, during that winter, DesBarres draws up the plans. He's come to the conclusion, I think, that he's not going to settle at Point Edward. I don't know why. It could be that he thought the water supply wasn't reliable enough. Crawley's Creek would be the main supply—but it does dry out—at least it does now—in the summer. The other possible place would be Leitches Creek, or Balls Creek. The problem with that is, it's not so defendable. It's a flat area. But Sydney Harbour, now, the peninsula, was different. It was built like Halifax peninsula, you see. You must remember, Muggah's Creek then was about ten times as wide as it is now. It's been filled in by slag from the steel plant. That's an important point—we always forget that. It was very wide at that time. So there was a very defensible peninsula, and a good supply of water from Wentworth Creek. And there was also a freshwater pond, no longer there, on the east side of the peninsula—what we call Louisa Gardens now.

In the spring, when the ice went out—I presume May—DesBarres and his son and a Loyalist by the name of David Tait, who had a background in surveying, came over, and they staked out what we today call the North End of Sydney. DesBarres drew up a plan which is one of the finest plans of any city in Canada. He hoped that Sydney would become one of the chief outposts of Britain in the New World. And he could see the potential in the coal fields and in the fish. Louisbourg had done it—why not Cape Breton? So he had very fond hopes.

He laid out the plans of a beautiful capital, with wide avenues, parks, a large commons area, circular drives where statues would presumably go, and a place for the government house, a large area at the north end for the military, which we call Victoria Park—it's still military there. A model like Bath, England—that idea of an eighteenth-century city, with fine curves. The plan of Sydney is magnificent; it's just beautiful when you look at it. It makes your mouth water. The streets are named after King George, Queen Charlotte, some members of the royal family. A member of the military is present to paint the portrait of the founding of Sydney, so we have a portrait of the *Blenheim* in the harbour. It's a capital city. Named after the head of the Colonial Office, Lord Sydney—Thomas

Townsend, Lord Sydney. As is Sydney, Australia. Sydney, Nova Scotia, is a few years older. So all of this shows the great hope that he had for the city, the ambition that he had for the city. And he names a street after himself—the first street is DesBarres. Good for him! And other members of the royal family, and military leaders. Lord Dorchester, who was the governor-general of Canada at the time, in Quebec.

He knew where the government house would be, and where the courthouse would be. And what they would look like. We have all the plans. He drew up a plan for a beautiful domed church in the round. That eventually, I think, transmogrified into St. George's round church in Halifax—which DesBarres helped plan.

Then, being a capital city, he brought the military—the 33rd Regiment. Arrived in the summer. They had been in New York. They came, and they helped further clear the land of trees and built their barracks—a beautiful barracks eventually went up at Victoria Park.

(*Do these people then move out of the barracks at Sydney Mines into the North End?*) Yes. They move into homes, a great number of them. A lot of them don't come into Sydney, of course. A lot of them are farmers. And they move over to what we call the Northwest Arm—that area from Upper North Sydney to Leitches Creek. The majority of the people, of course, are from backwoods New York state. And they immediately go into farming. They're not interested in coal mining or fishing. And of course, that land along the Northwest Arm is good land. Their descendants still live there—the Lewises, the Grandmeyers, the Allens. That whole area, you've got Loyalists.

The DesBarres people, the *Blenheim* people—many of them settled in Sydney, because they were carpenters and like that. But some of them went farming, too. But they tended to settle over in Westmount, in Point Edward—the Lewises and the Rudderhams, and Rudderhams, and Rudderhams, and Rudderhams. Just take a drive around there and you'll see. Most of those names that are there, even to this day— although you get a few obviously new names, the Eastern European names—generally speaking, they are descendants of the *Blenheim* crowd. Whereas the ones that settled on the Northwest Arm are descendants of the Loyalists. And in many cases, they maintained two establishments—one in the town, in Sydney, and one in the country. This is particularly true of the Upper Loyalists—Abraham Cuyler and David Matthews, who had been mayor of New York City. They lived at Point Edward, in Westmount.

(*DesBarres had a plan, he had an idea, he was in charge of the colony. Did it go smoothly?*) No. For DesBarres, it didn't go smoothly at all. Nothing in Cape Breton went smoothly. In this case what happened is, you've got a number of weaknesses that are bound to lead to trouble. You've got a Colonial Office who doesn't pay any money out. You've got people here—but the population in the immediate area of Sydney would probably number no more than 500 people, and therefore, they have very little power in England. Compared to the Loyalists in New Brunswick, where you have 35,000 at this time— powerful Loyalists. But our people are—there are not enough of them, they're not powerful enough. And therefore, they have very little say in the Colonial Office to try and get more money and more assistance. Moreover, the governor of Cape Breton was under the thumb, as it were, of the governor of Nova Scotia; this caused, in many cases, interference in the affairs of Cape Breton. If you didn't like your lieutenant-governor here in Cape Breton, you could easily cause trouble—if you were locally important like Cuyler or Matthews— by running off to the lieutenant-governor in Halifax and saying, "This fellow's making an awful mess."

(*And this happened to DesBarres?*) Oh, it happened to Des-

Barres, and it happened to a number of other governors. But it happened to DesBarres—very badly. DesBarres, for example, he appointed as his chief justice a very good friend of his, Richard Gibbons. Gibbons was from Halifax and had not got along with the Halifax establishment. They'd had a number of arguments—it's no use going into the reasons why, but there had been some terrible fights. And DesBarres appoints him chief justice of Cape Breton. Which just angers the people in Halifax to no end. And so when Mathews and Cuyler, particularly Cuyler, fight with DesBarres, trying to get power and DesBarres continually crushing him and not allowing him to get power—Cuyler runs off to these people in Halifax and makes up a number of stories about what DesBarres is doing, saying he's having illegal trade and that he's a dictator, and he's this, that, and the other thing. And they report this back to England. And to England it looks like the colony here is in chaos.

(At the same time, Cape Breton has no house of assembly.) That's right. And this makes it more difficult for a governor, because the Executive Council becomes, as it were, an assembly, fighting among themselves and bickering and arguing. In other words we have a lame colony, a lame constitution, an incomplete constitution. Can't tax. Can't pass laws. They pass laws, but legally, I guess, they shouldn't. They grant land. They can use the coal, and they do use the coal. But they're given no money to develop the mines. DesBarres tries to develop the mines on his own first, but he doesn't have the capital. And so he has to try to get private interests, and they don't have enough capital. He begins some mining, but really, it's unsuccessful. And as a result, he doesn't have enough money to run the government properly.

There's the anger of the Loyalists, trying to get their money back, as it were, and frustrated because they're not making money, because Britain isn't putting money to develop the colony. And they take it out on DesBarres. Des-

Barres is by nature a military man, an engineer—he's not a democrat, by any means. He fights with these people in Council, tries to tell them what to do. They won't listen to him, and they complain to Halifax. Halifax complains to London. London says to DesBarres, "Look, the mines are falling through, you're fighting with our Council, the place isn't taking off, people are leaving." Because many people that came begin to go. Things are moving along much better in New Brunswick, or in Canada, or in Nova Scotia.

Finally, Mathews and Cuyler get a number of their fellow Loyalists and some others, and they draw up a petition, a "remonstrance" as they call it, which they send to the Colonial Office, praying that DesBarres be removed. And they list a whole series of largely false accusations, I would say, against DesBarres. And he is called back to England by Lord Sydney to justify his situation.

DesBarres goes. And without even being formally dismissed, they appoint a new governor, Governor Macarmick. And this becomes the basis of DesBarres's next fight—that he wasn't properly dismissed, and that they owe him more money now for what they did to him. And this debate goes on for another twenty years. Twenty years! And it's partly on this basis that he's appointed lieutenant-governor of Prince Edward Island in 1804. As recompense for the Cape Breton mess; it's a mess on the part of the Colonial Office, especially. And they realize this. But by 1804 he's in his 80s. They're all dead—Lord Sydney is dead, everybody's dead. But they appoint him. And his Prince Edward Island sojourn is very successful. He learned from his problems in Cape Breton.

Just to go back, though—I think we have to really appreciate what DesBarres does. Supplies are scarce. The Colonial Office has literally forgotten us. Nova Scotia, Halifax, if anything, is an enemy of Sydney. They hate to see Nova Scotia cut up. And there's a movement in Nova Scotia that goes on for another 30, 40, 50 years, to try to make what they call "Nova Scotia Irredentia"—the old Nova Scotia, complete again. They don't like this diminution of their power. So they're always trying to get Cape Breton back—the governors and the merchants—particularly the coal mines. Eventually, they win, they do get it back. But at this period [1785-86] DesBarres is fighting them, and he's trying to get supplies. They send him no supplies. So he gives the supplies that are meant for Loyalists to the non-Loyalists who came on the *Blenheim*, because they're literally starving to death. But he's not supposed to do this; it's illegal. And Lord Sydney gets him on this—the legal aspect—which is just a ploy. And he can't deny this.

But on the other hand, he has to feed these people with Loyalist supplies. So bad is it that finally a ship runs aground at Arichat, and a group of them go off in sleighs that second winter, and they get the supplies and bring them back to Sydney—and that's what they feed the people. And the Indians feed the people the first winter with moosemeat and dogfish and this sort of thing, eels. I don't know if they could have survived without the assistance of the Indians the first winter. That's how difficult the situation was.

He kept his optimism, which is the mark of DesBarres, all the way through the whole thing. This colony could make it, it was great, everything was going strong. So he brings the settlers over, he feeds them, and begins the mining. He brings the first minister, Ranna Cossit, from New Hampshire—sells Ranna Cossit a bill of goods. Ranna Cossit goes back, gets his wife and family, and they build what we call Cossit House, and moves in as the first minister and the first teacher. Begins St. George's Church. Lays out the streets.

So the mark of DesBarres is everywhere. It's everywhere. Look at his maps, not just of Sydney but of the island at this period—you see he's planned out the first road to St. Peters, Lingan Road is planned out. He's already thinking in terms of the rest of the island. His mind is beyond just Sydney. And he writes about lumbering and mining and plaster of Paris and deer and fur skins and fishing. He's already thinking about the colony as a whole. Had he just stayed a few more years, he would have—being the kind of man he was—the great spirit that he was—he could have incorporated the whole island, and things would have been running, I think, much more smoothly. It took so much longer than it needs to have taken. But I think if DesBarres had been just given the chance, he would have had it going, let's say, ten years earlier.

(*How long did he have?*) Oh, less than two years. A terrible time. He left here. He couldn't land in England because his debtors were after him. Because, to pay for the supplies, he went on personal notes. (*Supplies that fed the starving people here.*) Yes. So when he left here, he couldn't go right to White-hall, right to the Colonial Office, to plead his case. He had to go to France, and go back to England in disguise, so that his debtors wouldn't know him, and sneak into the Colonial Office to plead his case. He got it all back, every penny. Twenty years. And about 8000 petitions.

(*And he outlived every one of them.*) Outlived! They were dead! He outlived his colony! (*Cape Breton was re-annexed to Nova Scotia in 1820.*) A lot of his children were dead. He outlived everybody. We're not quite sure when he was born. But the story they give is that he danced a jig on the table at the age of 100 in a Halifax tavern.

3

The Loyalists
of Cape Breton

THE LOYALISTS HAVE BEEN a relatively unknown group among the early settlers of Cape Breton. This is largely because their numbers were not great, they were swamped by the Scottish migration into the island, and because the political and social influence which they wielded in Sydney was destroyed when Cape Breton was annexed to Nova Scotia in 1820.

On the other hand, the Loyalists played a key role in the settlement of Cape Breton between 1784 and 1800. County capitals at Sydney, Port Hood and Baddeck, settlements of prime importance in the island's history, were founded by them. They held key offices there and greatly influenced the early political and social development of the island.

Since it deals with a largely unknown period in the history of Cape Breton, this essay will, of necessity, concentrate on the factual reconstruction of the settlement of the island's Loyalists. However, an attempt will be made to present an insight into their political and social influence in Sydney until annexation to Nova Scotia.

Between the fall of Louisbourg in 1758 and the arrival of the first Loyalists in 1784, Cape Breton was left undeveloped. Great Britain was unwilling to authorize land grants because mercantilistic theories forbade the development of the island's valuable coal deposits, which might lead to industrial competition with the mother country.[1] In 1768 the last troops were

31

withdrawn from Louisbourg for duty in Boston. This left behind about 300 Acadians, mostly on Isle Madame, together with about 400 Newfoundlanders, Irish and "Americans" who were allowed to practise the fishery, which required only minimal land use.[2]

The American Revolution made this policy of forbidding land grants in Cape Breton untenable, as thousands of land-hungry Loyalists began to flood into the remainder of British North America. By 1782, so many Loyalists were entering Quebec that the military governor, General Haldimand, began to look for suitable locations outside of the province in which to settle them.

For information on Nova Scotia he naturally turned to Samuel Holland, who had made a survey of Cape Breton between 1765 and 1767. Holland was enthusiastic about the possibilities of the island, "that with a little Encouragement wold [sic] invite Numbers to become Settlers."[3] Since 1779, he had been involved in surveying land for Loyalists in Quebec, and when asked by Haldimand about Cape Breton, he enthusiastically replied that the island would make an admirable "Asylum for the Refugees from the Sea Coasts of the Northern Provinces."[4]

While Haldimand was learning of Cape Breton's possibilities as a Loyalist refuge, Abraham Cuyler arrived in Quebec. Cuyler, former mayor of Albany, New York, had led a band of Loyalist volunteers in the American Revolution: for his loyalty he had lost £6,000 in real estate alone.[5] In compensation, he was appointed inspector of refugee Loyalists in Quebec. Perhaps as a result of discussion with Holland, he decided to lead a group of Loyalists to Cape Breton.[6]

Cuyler was a man of determination, and soon claimed that he had convinced 3,100 Loyalists to come with him to Cape Breton. One of these was Captain Jonathan Jones of the King's Rangers of New York, whom Cuyler commissioned to go to Cape Breton and explore likely settlement locations for Loyalists.[7] Jones left Quebec in the fall of 1783, but Cuyler, impatient with delay, and likely worried that his plans might fail without personal discussion with government officials, sailed for England in early November.

British officials had already given some thought to the settlement of Cape Breton: Lord North had turned to Joseph Frederick Wallet DesBarres for information. DesBarres had performed a hydrographical survey of the coast of Nova Scotia which he published as the *Atlantic Neptune* in 1783.[8] DesBarres had pointed out to Lord North the island's possibilities as a Loyalist settlement.[9]

When Cuyler arrived in early 1784, Thomas Townsend, Lord Sydney, was the home secretary. By then, there were rumours that Lord Sydney was planning a new political division of the Maritimes which would make Cape Breton a separate colony. He was assured by Cuyler that Loyalists were ready to settle there; Cuyler's only reservation lay in the cost of financing a new colonist establishment. Like North, he turned to DesBarres, who assured him that the government of the colony could operate on less than £2,500 per annum, and that the coal supply in Cape Breton could furnish nearby garrisons cheaply, employing Loyalists "without burthen to the Public."[10] The argument of settling Loyalists at minimal expense appealed to the financially burdened Pitt government and led directly to the establishment of the separate colony of Cape Breton. Sydney gave permission to Cuyler to bring his "Associated Loyalists" to Cape Breton.

Lord Sydney wrote Haldimand to allow the Associated Loyalists to leave Quebec for Louisbourg.[11] Disappointment was in store for Cuyler, however, for only 140 Loyalists arrived, the remainder having become discouraged that Cuyler would not be granted permission to settle Cape Breton. The Loyalists arrived at the end of October in three vessels, the brigs, *Liberty* and *Saint Peter*, and the schooner *Sally*. Two of the ships, one of which contained Jones and his followers, landed at St. Peters; the third with around forty heads of families continued on to Louisbourg where they met Cuyler. There were only four structures capable of providing the Loyalists with shelter in Louisbourg, and the governor of Nova Scotia, John Parr, beset with his own problems of Loyalist settlement, could offer them only locks and hinges.[12] Small comfort for this tiny group of Loyalists about to face a stormy, damp winter among the ruins of Louisbourg.

In the spring of 1785, the two shiploads of Loyalists who had landed at St. Peters went inland, and under Jonathan Jones established themselves on the Baddeck River. Jones was made magistrate for the Baddeck area and received 2,000 acres of land.

Other Loyalists came independently, some directly from the United States. Thus Captain David Smith came in his own ship from Massachusetts with his wife, one daughter and six sons. This family formed the backbone of settlement at Port Hood. Others stopped first in Nova Scotia before moving on to Cape Breton. A good example is Jacob Sparling who had received land in Shelburne County, and did not arrive in Cape Breton until 1808.[13]

While most of the Loyalists clustered around Baddeck, and eventually the Northwest Arm of Sydney Harbour, smaller groups settled near Ingonish, Port Hood and the Gut of Canso. It is difficult to estimate the number of Loyalists who came to Cape Breton, but using references in the Colonial Office records and early Cape Breton censuses and militia returns, it seems that no more than 500 such settlers came to the colony.

One reason for the difficulty in estimating the number of Loyalists who came to Cape Breton is that DesBarres never sent a record of their names to London. Consequently, settlers' lists include all pioneers [both Loyalist and non-Loyalist]. Abraham Cuyler did send in one return of Loyalists, however, claiming that there were 121 Loyalists with him in Sydney, including 44 adult males.[14] It is possible that the remaining 19 settlers of the 140 he claimed came with him were divided between St. Peters under Lieutenant Neil Robertson and Baddeck under Captain Jones. Land petition records from St. Peters and Baddeck certainly fail to point to more than this number. Terrence McCorristine, agent for the Loyalists from Quebec, claimed that only 37 Loyalists (probably adult males) came as a result of Cuyler's efforts, and 24 through the Quartermaster General's Department in Montreal. In all, he estimated only 81 Loyalists arrived, though this likely referred only to the Sydney area.[15] If we take Port Hood, the Margaree area, and the Miras together, we might possibly reach 200 people. Richard Brown in his *A History of the Island of Cape Breton* (1869) estimated that 800 people arrived,[16] but this number was probably derived from Cuyler's request for provisions for 500 families made in 1784.[17] Together with DesBarres's settlers, it is likely that no more than 300 to 400 people came to Cape Breton during the first few years of its colonial existence.

THROUGHOUT THE PERIOD of their greatest influence, before 1820, the Loyalist families intermarried with a high degree of regularity, even though Scots in large numbers were living nearby. Hence the Harts and the Ingrahams of Margaree intermarried, as did the Ingrahams and Leavers of Baddeck. The Ingrahams and Harts were both justices of the peace for their areas, and the Leavers were important merchants. This story can be repeated for the Daisleys and Wilhausens, the Peters and Meloneys, the Peters and the Watsons,[18] the Paynes and the Spencers.[19] Often the families lived distances apart for those days of difficult travel. Yet, their in-

termarriages were common and resulted in the growth of locally influential families.

The picture painted thus far is that of a small, typically
Loyalist community, not unlike that of parts of New Brunswick at the period. However, the Loyalists of Cape Breton experienced competition from British settlers early in their history. First, when the lieutenant-governor of the new colony, J.
F. W. DesBarres, received his appointment, he collected 129
settlers including disbanded soldiers and tradesmen, who
sailed aboard the 600-ton *Blenheim*, arriving at Louisbourg 5
November 1784. There they met Cuyler and his Loyalists,
then sailed to Spanish Harbour, landing at Point Edward 24
November.[20]

Immediately a dichotomy was established. DesBarres and
his settlers organized themselves in the new colonial capital at
Sydney; Cuyler and his Loyalists were forced to leave Louisbourg for Sydney in the spring of 1785. The enmity between
DesBarres and Cuyler, between British and Loyalist settler,
dates from this period. The Loyalist hand was somewhat
strengthened by the arrival of more of their number, some of
whom were of great influence, after 1785. The chief of these
was David Mathews, former mayor of New York City. He had
lost a good deal of property as a result of the American Revolution and was determined to make up his losses.[21] Mathews was
to serve as attorney-general of the colony and act as senior
councillor. Cuyler was secretary and registrar. These were the
two most influential positions outside of that of lieutenant-
governor.

The power of Mathews and of Cuyler was also enhanced
by the fact that the colony lacked a house of assembly. Britain
had decided to wait to grant the assembly until the island
should attain a higher population.[22] Hence the Executive
Council became the centre for political expression and a
forum for debate. This in turn led to divisions which stymied

the work of the colonial executive; it also emphasized the social cleavage already present in Sydney. The composition of the Council reflected this division. In 1790 David Mathews and Abraham Cuyler occupied seats along with the Loyalist, Ingraham Ball, and Benjamin Lovell, the Loyalist troop chaplain from Massachusetts. The non-Loyalists were Archibald Charles Dodd who came from England in 1787, Thomas Crawley, former naval captain, and William Smith, surgeon for the 33rd Regiment. In general, the Council divided in its opinions between these two groups.

These divisions can best be illustrated with three important examples involving the apportionment of food supplies, the removal of DesBarres, and the development of political organizations in Sydney.

Cape Breton as a small colony was subordinate to Nova Scotia, in that the lieutenant-governor of that province might assume control of Cape Breton if bodily present on the island. As far as supplies for the Loyalists were concerned, they were sent to Major General Campbell, commanding the forces in Halifax, for distribution to troops and Loyalists. The supplies were in turn sent to Major Yorke of the 33rd Regiment stationed in Sydney. DesBarres, like Thomas Carleton, lieutenant-governor of New Brunswick, objected to this arrangement, fearing that it cut into his powers. Moreover, it is possible that DesBarres was trying to supply non-Loyalist settlers with food supplies meant for the Loyalists alone.[23] This would account for the fact that DesBarres never sent a selective list of settlers to London.

When DesBarres tried to seize control of supplies, open conflict broke out in the colony. Cuyler, Mathews and the Loyalists in the Sydney area who came with Cuyler supported Yorke.[24] DesBarres appears to have been backed by a majority of the other settlers. The Council was split; Lovell and Mathews left. When Yorke tried to ease the situation by allowing

DesBarres to distribute some of the supplies, Cuyler antagonised him by saying Council was laughing at him for being hoodwinked out of the supplies by DesBarres.[25] Contention rose again, and was calmed only by DesBarres' purchasing supplies on his own account.

These incidents not only widened the division between the Loyalists and the other settlers, but led directly to the removal of DesBarres. Cuyler drew up a "Remonstrance and Petition" in which he condemned DesBarres' conduct as "painful to British-born Subjects."[26] He was supported in this by Mathews, Lovell and, of course, Yorke. This resulted directly in DesBarres' removal.

The squabble over the control of supplies, which was rooted in the two groups that first settled Sydney, led not only to the removal of DesBarres but to the establishment of rival political organizations within the colony. These organizations developed even though the colony was without a house of assembly, and revealed the split between Loyalist and non-Loyalist. First, just before DesBarres left Sydney he had unofficially sanctioned the formation of volunteer militia, mainly for his supporters' protection against the 33rd Regiment. Chief Justice Richard Gibbons[27] used this as the nucleus of a "Friendly Society" which "held nightly meetings of the lower order of men...."[28] It is plain that the Society was composed of settlers from the *Blenheim*.

Mathews was behind the formation of another association made up, according to Lieutenant-Governor Macarmick, of "all the principal people, that I might be obliged to fill vacancies out of this society."[29] Macarmick crushed both groups, even though Mathews was infuriated at anyone's impeaching his loyalty.[30] Though the membership of the attorney-general's group was never spelled out, it would hardly have been composed of the *Blenheim* group whom Mathews described as "the Mob."[31]

A closer analysis of these two groups reveals that not all of the Loyalists were followers of Cuyler and Mathews. Generally speaking, those who arrived with Cuyler formed a united group, but those who arrived after 1785 either were not admitted to Cuyler's clique or were won over by DesBarres and his followers. Among these were Ranna Cossit of New Hampshire, the first Anglican minister in Sydney, and William McKinnon who was a southern Loyalist. After the removal of DesBarres and the death of Richard Gibbons, Ranna Cossit became leader of Mathew's enemies, and for six years, between 1794 and 1800, these two Loyalists fought for political and social control of the colony.

Council was the scene of constant conflict, and the colony was the despair of its administrators.[32] The second lieutenant-governor, William Macarmick, had to strengthen his position, which had been weakened by the dismissal of DesBarres. Consequently, he drove Cuyler from the colony in 1793, greatly diminishing the Loyalist influence. However, at Macarmick's retirement in 1795, Mathews, as senior councillor, became administrator, dismissing Cossit and his followers from Council. Finally, in 1799 John Murray became administrator and destroyed Mathews' power, dismissing him from his position of attorney-general and removing his supporters from Council. Cossit and his group supported Murray, of course, so that by 1800, when Murray left Cape Breton, Cossit was in effect leader of the Council.

These Loyalist divisions affected not only Sydney's political life, but reached into religion and education as well. Since there was no house of assembly in the colony, and since Ranna Cossit was deeply involved in political events in the colony, vestry meetings at St. George's Church, Sydney's first house of worship, were scenes of deep divisions which generally followed political lines. Entries in the Church Registry, like this one for 13 April 1789, give hints of division:

"At a meeting of the parish on this Day for the purpose of choosing Church Wardens and vestry men, Mr. More [*sic*] proposed Mr. D. Mathews Esq'r and Mr. A. Cuyler Esq'r for Ch'h Wardens, the former being unanimously objected to, instead of whom he proposed Mr. Dodd."[33]

Mathews was defeated in his other bid for position of church warden and stopped attending church.[34] In another case, remarks made by members of the rival factions at a church meeting practically precipitated a duel.[35]

In education Ranna Cossit, as minister, was to have charge of choosing teachers, but Mathews and his fellow Loyalists refused to send their children to Cossit's teacher, favouring instead a man of the Roman Catholic faith.[36]

These divisions hurt the colony in almost every way until the two chief protagonists, Mathews and Cossit, were removed from the scene, the former by death in 1800, and the latter by Bishop Inglis who made a special trip from Halifax to induce the controversial cleric to leave Sydney, where his involvement in politics had become a scandal which might lead people to becoming "Methodists, Catholics, or infidels."[37] Cossit was transferred to Yarmouth.

The removal of these two Loyalists coincided with the arrival of the tide of Scottish settlers into the island. Between 1802 and 1820 the population grew from around 2,000 to over 9,000. The Loyalists outside of Sydney were swamped by the Gaels, though they continued to retain positions of local influence. Since the Scots were mainly farmers, fishermen or shipbuilders, they were not attracted to town life. Consequently, only a small proportion of them came to Sydney before the development of the coal mines by the General Mining Association in 1827.

However, their presence affected Sydney indirectly. With the arrival of so many new settlers in the colony, a move for a legislative assembly developed led by Richard Gibbons Jr., son of the first chief justice.[38] In order to achieve their goal, Gibbons and his followers claimed that since the colony had no house of assembly the collection of a duty on rum, inaugurated in 1801, was unconstitutional. However, since the colony needed an income, the simplest answer was the granting of a house of assembly. The followers of Cossit seem to have endorsed Gibbons' movement, while Mathews' group seems to have fallen under the leadership of A. C. Dodd, an Englishman who became chief justice of the colony. He opposed Gibbons' group, calling them "restless spirits."[39]

The political situation in Sydney after 1802 is thus dominated by Cossit and then Gibbons, who were supported by the majority of settlers, and Dodd, who seemed to have held the support of Mathews' followers, largely Loyalists. As the years went on, however, more and more of the Loyalists joined Gibbons, so that by 1816 the administrator, Colonel Jonas Fitzherbert, declared that Gibbons' support centred on former Americans.[40] If this is true, it is possible that most of the Loyalists supported an assembly, and were joining Gibbons.

Matters came to a head in 1816 when Ranna Cossit Jr., assistant customs collector and supporter of Gibbons, refused to collect the rum duty. R. J. Uniacke Jr., the attorney-general, claimed that the move had a wide spectrum of support.[41] Cossit was forced to begin collecting again, but merchants Ritchie and Leaver, who ran the coal mines, refused to pay back duties. The case was taken to court by the Crown, and it was decided that the tax was illegal since the colony had no house of assembly.[42]

The reaction of the Colonial Office was a surprise to the colonists, for instead of granting a house of assembly, it decided to re-annex the colony to Nova Scotia. This simply brought all parties together in a display of unity, that Lieutenant-Governor Ainslie said was "Yankee." Besides this, Ainslie considered them "the refuse of the three Kingdoms."[43] Annex-

41

ation, however, was inevitable, and Lieutenant-Governor
Kempt of Nova Scotia arrived in Sydney 16 October 1820 to
claim his colony's new possession.

With annexation to Nova Scotia, the importance of the
Cape Breton Loyalist diminished. Neither of the island's first
representatives in Halifax was a Loyalist. As time passed, inter-
marriage between Loyalist and Scot dimmed any sense of Loyalist exclusiveness. In Baddeck and Sydney a realization of
Loyalist background remains, but in Sydney the blending of
Loyalist and *Blenheim* families has resulted in confusion as to
just who is a Loyalist. The fact that DesBarres and Cuyler kept
no records designating Loyalists adds to the problem. However, most Loyalists are aware of their ancestry. J. G. McKinnon noted that the first two mayors after Sydney's incorporation as a city were both descendants of John Meloney,
Sydney's first Loyalist settler.[44] Recent publications outline
family connections fully and assure a continuing record of
Loyalist families among Cape Bretoners.[45]

What kind of person was the Cape Breton Loyalist? Generally, he was either an official, a farmer or a soldier from
northern New England. There are few records of first-
generation Loyalists taking part in trade, either in running the
coal mines, in shipbuilding or in ocean trade. They seem to
have come seeking land or office, and it seems that many left
in the first difficult years after the establishment of the colony,
which did not really begin to prosper until large numbers of
Scots arrived.

The Cape Breton Loyalist does not seem to have been a
political innovator. The move for a house of assembly came
from Richard Gibbons, whose father was a pre-Loyalist from
Halifax. While the Loyalists were intensely politically-
minded—men like Cuyler, Mathews, Cossit and McKinnon
are prime examples—they seem to have been interested in
maintaining their social and political positions rather than in

gaining more rights and responsibilities. The chief danger of a house of assembly was that it would lessen their political power.

The preceding may seem a harsh judgment of the Cape Breton Loyalists. If the colony had been granted a house of assembly and had not been annexed to Nova Scotia in 1820, it is possible that the factions led by Cuyler and Mathews or by Cossit and Gibbons would have evolved into political parties allowing Cape Breton to contribute to the growth of British institutions in America. The small colony of Prince Edward Island witnessed the rise of a Loyalist society much like Mathews', which was elected to the house of assembly and "prepared the way for the development of democratic government in Prince Edward Island."[46] In Cape Breton, where there was no house of assembly, Mathews' and Cossit's groups simply fought to no apparent end, to the despair of politician and settler alike.

Despite their small numbers and their eclipse after 1820, the Cape Breton Loyalists are of interest, since they found themselves in somewhat different circumstances from their counterparts in Nova Scotia, New Brunswick and Canada. A grasp of their history contributes to a deeper understanding of that complex creature we call the Loyalist.

LIST OF CAPE BRETON LOYALISTS

The following list of Cape Breton Loyalists was composed using various documents including victualling lists, correspondence and a few family histories. Since the Cape Breton authorities failed to draw up lists of Loyalists as such, a great deal of cross-checking was necessary. In most cases the author has relied on documentary evidence for names and information. The two exceptions are the names Severence and Sheperd for which there are strong family traditions of Loyalist ancestry but no documentary evidence as yet. The author would appreciate any information available on any Cape Breton Loyalist in order to make this list more complete and exact.

NAME	ORIGIN	LOCATION IN CAPE BRETON	OTHER INFORMATION
ALCOCK, Nathan		North West Arm, Sydney Harbour	23rd Regiment
ALLEN, Jeremiah		North West Arm,	

NAME	ORIGIN	LOCATION IN CAPE BRETON	OTHER INFORMATION
c. 1726-1809		Sydney Harbour	
ANDERSON, John			
ANTELL, John (Major)			
AYMOR, Mary		Sydney	Husband - John
BAINE, John		Sydney	74th Regiment
BALL, Ingram 1752-1807	b. Gloucester, England	Ball's Creek, arrived 1788	Captain, 7th Dragoons; Wife & 6 children; Estate Oak Farm, 1000 acres.
BATTERSBY, John		Sydney River	38th Regiment
BEYERS, Jacob			
BLACKEY, John		Sydney	82nd Regiment
BOISSEAU, James E.	South Carolina	Sydney	Estate: Indian Cove, 600 acres - called "Fair Forest"
BRADLEY, Patrick		North West Arm, Sydney Harbour	23rd Regiment
BROOKS, John		Sydney	
BROWN, William		Sydney	Single; carpenter
BUELL, William	Virginia	Baddeck, arrived 1785	Ensign
BUTTERWORTH, William 1786-		Gut of Canso (Ship Harbour)	Cooper
CAIN,		Baddeck	
CAMERON, John (Lieut.)		Liverpool, N.S. to Spanish River 1783	King's Orange Rangers
CAMERON, Kenneth		Sydney, Little Pond	74th Regiment
CARTER, Joseph 1743-		Gut of Canso	
CLARK, Peter		Shelburne, N.S. to Englishtown, Leitches Creek	
CLARKE, Job B.	Rhode Island	Sydney	
CLARKE, Joseph (John?)		Sydney	38th Regiment
COSSIT, Ranna (Rev.) -1815	New Hampshire	Sydney-Louisbourg Road; arrived 1787	First permanent Protestant minister in C.B. Wife & 10 children
CUYLER, Abraham	Mayor, Albany, New York	North West Arm, Sydney Harbour	Estate: Yorkfields
DAISLEY, William	Rhode Island	Cape North	
DAVIS, Benjamin			
DAY, William 1739-	New York	Sydney; arrived 1785	
DEANE, Nicholas		Sydney	
DENNY, Dennis		Sydney	22nd Regiment
DICKSON, Alexander			
DIXON, Robert			82nd Regiment
EAGEN (EGAN), John			Single; carpenter
ELDER, Alexander			33rd Regiment
FENTON, James		Sydney	
FERRES, Joseph (Lieut.)	New York	Gabarus, 1784-1786	Farmer; blacksmith carpenter; served in Revolutionary War; Wife & 4 children
FOYLE, Henry		Baddeck	
FRASER, Alex		Sydney	33rd Regiment
FRASER, Colin			33rd Regiment
FRASER, Thomas			33rd Regiment
GARDINER, John		Sydney	74th Regiment
GAY, James			
GOOLD, James 1775-	States	Baddeck, 1790	
GRANDMEYER, John Christian, 1753-1846		North West Arm, Sydney Harbour	Hessian
GRANT, Gregory		Sydney	72nd Regiment

44

NAME	ORIGIN	LOCATION IN CAPE BRETON	OTHER INFORMATION
GRANT, Peter	New York		Carpenter
GRAY, Samuel 1776-		Port Hood	Shoe-maker
HAIRE, Alexander	New York?	Sydney, Mira	Commissaire of C.B. Loyalists
HAMILTON, John		Sydney	82nd Regiment
HAMILTON, Samuel			
HART, Josiah	Connecticut	Manchester, N.S. to Margaree 1783	
HAWLEY, Mathew (Capt.) 1749-	Connecticut	Guysborough to Port Hood 1789, to Mabou	Cooper
HEFFRON, Michael			Ship Pilot in U.S. Revolution
HENRY, John			
HICKEY, Edward		Sydney	
HIGGINS, John (Capt) b. Ireland 1744	New York	Gut of Canso (Plaister Cove)	Land Surveyor; School-master; Wife & 2 children
HILL, Robert		North West Arm, Sydney Harbour	Royal Artillery
HOMES (HOLMES), James - 1773-		Gut of Canso	Farmer
HULL, Henry	Connecticut	Guysborough, Baddeck	
INGRAHAM, Hezekiah 1755-	Connecticut	Margaree Harbour via Hfx., Guysboro 1783	First J.P. at Margaree Harbour
INGRAHAM, James 1780-		Baddeck, Margaree 1791	Son of Hezekiah; Cooper
JAMES, David		Sydney	7th Regiment?
JEFFERSON, Joseph (James?) 1768-1833	Virginia	North West Arm, Sydney Harbour	80th Regiment
JENNER, Thomas			
JONES, David	New York; b. Connecticut		7th Regiment
JONES, Francis		Sydney	
JONES, Jonathan	New York; b. Connecticut	Baddeck	Loyal Rangers; Wife & 5 children
KELLY, John	Pennsylvania		84th Regiment; Single
KING, Ausberry c. 1768-	Virginia	To N.S. 1784 to Gut of Canso, 1797	Farmer
KING, Barry 1768-		Gut of Canso	
KING, Edward 1770-	Boston	Mabou	Farmer; single (Married by 1818)
KING, Henry 1762-		Ship Harbour 1785 via N.S.	Farmer; fisherman; married, 7 children by 1818
KING, John			
LARREBY, John 1764-	New England	Mabou	
LEAVER, John	New York	Baddeck	Wife dead; 7 children
LEITCH, John		Leitches Creek Bras d'Or	Royal Carolina Regiment
LEWIS, Henry c. 1758-	Virginia	Leitches Creek	
LINDEN, Henry 1763-		Gut of Canso	Farmer
LLOYD, Pat			
LLOYD, Thomas		Sydney	
LORWAY, Richard 1755-	Albany, New York	Louisbourg 1781	Single
LOVELL, Benjamin (Rev.) 1755-1828	Massachusetts	South West Arm, Sydney Harbour	

NAME	ORIGIN	LOCATION IN CAPE BRETON	OTHER INFORMATION
MCCORRISTINE, Terrence	New York	Sydney	Merchant; Wife & 3 children
MCDONALD, John			
MCGILVERY, Daniel		Low Point, arrived 1785	
MCGREGOR, Daniel	New York		Farmer; single
MCKAY, Robert			
MCKENZIE, Paul			33rd Regiment
MCKINNON, William -1817	Carolina; b. Scotland	Sydney	
MANN, Isaac	New York	Baddeck, arrived 1785	
MANNING, William 1775-		Mabou	
MARPLE, Richard		N.E. Margaree	
MARSLAND, William		Sydney	23rd Regiment
MARTIN, John		North West Arm, Sydney Harbour	
MATHEWS, David -1800	Mayor, New York City	North West Arm, Sydney Harbour	Estate: Point Amelia
MELONEY, John D.	Long Island, N.Y.	Sydney, arrived 1784	Wife & 3 children
MIDDLETON, William			33rd Regiment
MOFFAT, James	Rhode Island	North West Arm, Sydney Harbour	
MOLYNEUX, Stephen		Sydney	
MOORE, Adam		Leitches Creek	
MOORE, George 1748-	b. Ireland	Great Arichat	10 yrs. as naval officer; single
MOOREHEAD, John		Sydney	
MURRAY, John d. 1797		Sydney	63rd Regiment; son-in-law of D. Mathews?
MUSGRAVE Bartholomew 1757-1837	New York	North West Arm, Sydney Harbour	
NEAL, Henry			
NESTOR, James		Sydney	King's Orange Rangers
O'BRIEN, John		Sydney	
OWENS, Francis		Sydney	
PAYNE, P.		Mira	
PERRY, Henry Widimore		Sydney	
PETERS, John (Lt. Col.) 1740 -1788	Connecticut; J.P. in New York	Baddeck; Upper North Sydney	Wife & 6 children
PLANT, William 1775-	New York	Upper North Sydney	
RAY, James	New York	North West Arm, Sydney Harbour	76th Regiment
REYNOLDS, Stephen 1763-		To N.S. 1784, then to Gut of Canso 1797	Farmer
RICHARDS, Jesse		Sydney	
ROBERTS, Henry		Sydney	
ROBERTSON, Neil (Lt.)	New York	St. Peters Baddeck; Ship Hbr.	Royal Rangers
ROPER, John 1772-1837	Norfolk, Virginia	Port Hood, 1788, to Ingonish, 1823	
ROSS, Alexander			33rd Regiment
ROSS, David			33rd Regiment
RUDGE, Benjamin		Sydney	Royal Artillery
SCYTES, D.			
SEVERENCE		Forchu	
SHANNAHAN, John		Sydney	
SHEPERD		Mira	
SMITH, David (Capt.) 1742-1789	Massachusetts	Port Hood 1786	Wife - Rebecca
SMITH, David 1775-1851	Massachusetts	Port Hood	Son of Capt. David
SMITH, Harding 1783-	Massachusetts	Port Hood	Son of Capt. David
SMITH, Isaac 1780-1853	Massachusetts	Port Hood (also Mabou)	Son of Capt. David; Trader

NAME	ORIGIN	LOCATION IN CAPE BRETON	OTHER INFORMATION
SMITH, John		Sydney	
SMITH, Lewis 1771-1846	Massachusetts	Port Hood (also Mabou)	Son of Capt. David; Farmer
SMITH, Lewis 1777-		Mabou	
SMITH, Parker 1781-1851	Massachusetts	Port Hood	Son of Capt. David; Farmer
SPARLING, Jacob 1770-	New York	North Sydney	
SPENCER, John	New Hampshire b. Connecticut	Mira in 1786	
STEWART, John		Sydney	80th Regiment
STEWART, Robert			
STOREY, John		Sydney; Canso	
SUTHERLAND, John		Sydney	7th Regiment
SUTHERLAND, Alex			33rd Regiment
STAFFORD, William	Maryland	Sydney in 1798	
SWAIN, Benjamin		Sydney	38th Regiment
TAIT, David 1740-1834	West Florida, Carolina	Sydney, Mira River	Single
TAYLOR, John			
TUTTLE, Ebenezer	New York		Farmer; single
UPTON, John 1751-		River Inhabitants	Prov. Regiment
WATSON, Daniel W.	New York	Point Edward	
WATSON, John	New York	Sydney	Fisherman; single
WATSON, William 1775-	New York	Baddeck in 1788	Son of Daniel
WATTS, Hugh	South Carolina	Little Judique to Port Hood, 1784	
WEHMAN, H.			King's Orange Rangers Trader
WHEATON, John 1753-		Gut of Canso (Plaister Cove)	
WHEELER, Lydia		Baddeck River in 1786	Wife of James Edward Boisseau
WHITNEY, Josiah 1745-		Gut of Canso	Fisherman; married 1818
WILHAUSEN, Frederick		North West Arm, Sydney Harbour to Englishtown	Hessian Regt. of Louisbourg?
WORTH, Benjamin 1754-	New Jersey	Mabou in 1786	
YOUNG, Reuben 1759[8?]		Mabou	

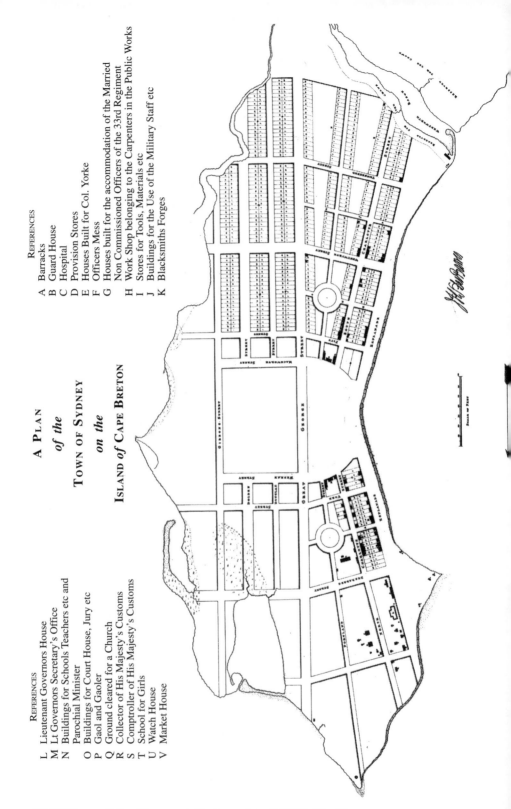

A PLAN

of the

TOWN OF SYDNEY

on the

ISLAND of CAPE BRETON

1786 Plan of the Town of Sydney by J.F.W. DesBarres

4

Early Surveyors of Cape Breton

A TALK

SURVEYING is one of the earliest professions recorded in Cape Breton. This is partly because of the island's position as a stepping-off place for Europe; seamen wanted to know the positions and depths of the safest harbours and where exactly the island lay in relation to Europe. Later, since the island was one of the first places in Canada to be settled by Europeans and subsequently to gain importance in inter-imperial warfare, it had to be accurately surveyed. Finally, after the heat of battle died down, in the nineteenth century many thousands of Loyalist and Scottish settlers had to be located and their lands accurately surveyed. Hence over the years Cape Breton's surveyors have had to locate the island accurately, then define its coasts clearly, describe its interior, and finally demarcate land grants. This process took a little over a century and involved some outstanding names in Canada's surveying history.

I thought that today I might illustrate this fascinating period between approximately 1750 and 1850 with a brief look at the careers of four surveyors of this island: Joseph-Bernard Chabert de Cogolin, Samuel Holland, Joseph Frederick Wallet DesBarres and Captain Thomas Crawley.

Joseph-Bernard Chabert de Cogolin, popularly known as Chabert, was a native of Toulon, France, and as a navy man entered a career as a navigator who found himself off the coasts of Nova Scotia when the French tried to regain Louisbourg after its first fall in 1745. The attempt was a failure, and Chabert claimed that the charts giving the location of Cape Breton were inaccurate. Consequently, when Louisbourg was regained by France at the peace table, Chabert was sent there to determine the accurate position of the island. Chabert brought with him a quadrant, "equipped with a telescope divided by transversals and by points, and furnished with a micrometer [and] telescopes of various sizes" as well as other instruments. There were so many telescopes that in 1750 Chabert built an observatory in the governor's garden, which was likely Canada's first observatory. Plotting the stars, and using as exact measurements for distance as possible, in 1753 Chabert published a 288-page report entitled *Voyage Fait Par Ordre Du Roi en 1750 et 1751*. It was the first attempt to locate what is today the province of Nova Scotia with scientific accuracy.

After the second and final fall of Louisbourg, Great Britain assumed control of Cape Breton in 1763. She was determined to retain the island because of its strategic location near the valuable fishery at the mouth of the St. Lawrence River. More important, she wanted to know about her new real estate; she knew there was coal, but how much? She knew there was good land, but where? She lost no time in appointing one of the great surveyors of the eighteenth century, Samuel Holland, to give her an accurate description of the island. Holland was appointed in 1764 and, using what was left of Louisbourg as his headquarters, surveyed the island until 1767. Holland had an illustrious career before surveying Cape Breton. A Dutchman by birth, he had later moved to England and like many surveyors of his day served in the military with the army. His work in the New World involved a map of New York Colony; he served at the second siege of Louisbourg and made a plan of the town and the environs of the former fortress town; he then went to Saint John where he supervised the erection of Fort Frederick; then to Quebec with Wolfe where he was appointed surveyor-general of Quebec and the Northern District of America in 1764. It was in this position that he surveyed Cape Breton.

Holland organized three surveying parties for different parts of the island but compiled them himself in one *Description*. He was the first to divide the island into counties and townships, some of whose names still survive, such as Port Hood, but most of which were superseded by older names of the French or Mi'kmaq. However, the accuracy of his surveys and the orderliness of his observations are beyond dispute and his maps, now rare, and located, in all places, in Ann Arbor, Michigan, indicate that his surveys were the most accurate to date while his estimate of the great potential of the fishing, gypsum, coal and lumbering industries on the island have been borne out for two centuries.

A list of some of the instruments at Holland's disposal indicates the extreme simplicity of the technology of his period in history, and includes an astronomical clock "with a Compounded Pendulum, and a Spring to keep it going when the Clock is wound up," a quadrant of two feet radius, a two-foot Gregorian reflecting telescope, and a ten-foot refracting telescope.

In order to gauge accurately the degree of longitude which by then was the most pressing need for navigators, Holland observed the passage of Jupiter's satellites and observed with accuracy the passage of Venus between the sun and the earth. Using the accurate clocks he had with him and comparing the times of the transit with those made by fellow surveyors in England, he was able to deduct with the greatest accuracy to date the distance between Cape Breton and Europe and by implication its approximate longitude in relation to England. Samuel Holland's work, not only in Cape Breton but also in New York, Prince Edward Island and Quebec, set a standard which has hardly been surpassed in dispassionate accurate surveying, in scientific observation, and in surprising disinterestedness when it came to financial and personal gain.

How different from our next figure, the flamboyant, irascible genius Joseph Frederick Wallet DesBarres! It is impossible in this brief paper to describe the personal entanglements of this man's long life. Suffice it to say that his contests with governments, women, his nineteen children, and tenants on his far-flung lands could fill volumes. He surveyed thousands of miles of coastline, governed two colonies, laid out dockyards, surveyed the St. Lawrence with Captain Cook, was present at the fall of Louisbourg and of Quebec, surveyed the principal ports of Newfoundland, surveyed the fortifications of New York, and built a castle. Despite this breathtaking pace he found time and had the artistic genius to produce some of the most beautiful views that we have of the east coast of North America. These were published in 1783 as the *Atlantic Neptune* and are the works of an artist as much as those of a surveyor. It is on this aspect of DesBarres's career that I will say a few words.

As the war clouds gathered over the Thirteen Colonies after the fall of Louisbourg, Britain began to realize that if conflict should erupt, she would need an accurate survey of the coasts of North America to determine the safest places for warships to sail and dock. With Samuel Holland preoccupied with his description of Cape Breton and Prince Edward Island, DesBarres, who might otherwise have been superseded, stepped forth. Never a shy person, DesBarres, though [probably] of Swiss birth, claimed an impressive career serving under the British. Moreover, the magnitude of the project and the few resources Britain was willing to devote to such a huge undertaking frightened away more timid souls.

DesBarres had to beg and borrow vessels and find his own crews. On the positive side, however, great advances were being made in hydrography in the late eighteenth century. The theodolite had been refined and the quadrant, which is the forerunner of the sextant and the chronometer, were in use. DesBarres also employed the newly-developed technique of triangulation for measuring distances between points of land. This meant that shorelines could be accurately plotted and soundings could be accurately positioned.

For the ten years between 1763 and 1773 DesBarres spent his summers in the dangerous task of surveying the coasts of the Western Atlantic and his winters drawing up his charts at his home at Castle Frederick in Falmouth, Nova Scotia. Though he nearly lost his life off Sable Island, DesBarres persevered, and between 1777 and 1784 published his famous *Atlantic Neptune* in four editions. These editions included not only charts but beautiful, elegant, artistic views of various shorelines complete with people, ships, buildings and the magnificence of the natural surroundings. The *Neptune* was not only beautiful, but was praised for its accuracy, since it was far superior to any charts of the east coast of North America previously published. Indeed, the charts were used until the late nineteenth century.

Though DesBarres had achieved a masterpiece of surveying he had neglected to keep accurate accounts, and spent twenty-five years trying to get recompense from the Board of Trade, since he had been responsible for and had had to justify each expense. This wrangle DesBarres blamed for his lack of promotion, and he had enough influence to receive in partial recompense the appointment of lieutenant-governor of Cape Breton when it was made a separate colony in 1784.

The scope of this paper does not allow us to examine his role as politician and founder of Sydney, nor his later career as lieutenant-governor of Prince Edward Island. However, his appointment as founder of a new colony did allow him to give full vent to his career of surveyor. Through the winter of 1784-85 he planned a fine capital for his new colony. Streets would be laid out in regular order together with broad avenues, a fine

Esplanade along the waterfront, with parks and views. This would be Sydney, named after Thomas Townsend, Lord Sydney, then secretary of state for the colonies. The plan was Georgian, but many of his ideas were later adapted by town planners in the nineteenth century. More than Sydney, however, DesBarres envisioned a whole network of satellite communities with Sydney as the geometric nucleus linked to these settlements by a series of boulevards. Each satellite was to be circular in form with a circular plaza in the middle. Four roads would radiate out from each town, with lots, which were successively larger in size, strung out along them. The satellite towns would be located at various distances from Sydney; Friendstown, the nearest, was five miles away, Pittsburg was four miles further, while St. Peters was seven miles away. Surveying actually took place and some lots were granted to conform to this plan. Indeed there is still a right-of-way in existence for the road to St. Peters which cuts across part of modern Sydney and its suburbs. Unfortunately, DesBarres's plan was never carried out, but if it had been, one town planner has claimed that it would have been the only imaginatively planned project in eighteenth-century Nova Scotia.

Some of DesBarres's plans for Sydney were carried out, however. The grid pattern of the historic North End of the city, with the broad sweep of George Street, the location of the military lands, as well as the street names of that section of town, testify to the original plan of this great surveyor. One need only contrast the North End with town development during the early twentieth century in parts of Sydney like Ashby or Whitney Pier to realize the genius of DesBarres. With its historic buildings and orderly layout along the harbour, the North End has become a desirable residential section of modern Sydney.

After DesBarres left Cape Breton, less well-known surveyors followed. Men like Thomas Hurd and Alexander Haire laid out the first land grants for the Loyalists who came to the Sydney area. One of these, however, Thomas Crawley, stands out as one of Nova Scotia's greatest surveyors. Crawley, whose name is memorialized at Crawley's Creek across the harbour from Sydney, where the Canadian Coast Guard College is now located, was born in 1757 and was a native of Ipswich, England. He spent his early life in the Royal Navy during the Revolutionary War and later served under Admiral Nelson. He left the navy as a captain and was always known as "Captain Crawley."

Crawley found his way to Cape Breton by 1788 where he was appointed to the Colonial Council. He was always a well-respected individual despite the partisan bickering that characterized the life of the young colony, and served as major in the local militia, superintendent of the mines and justice of the peace. In 1805, he was appointed surveyor-general of Cape Breton, a position he held until at least 1834. This term coincided with a huge influx of 30,000 Scots who came to settle on the island, as well as hundreds of Acadians from St. Pierre and Miquelon who moved to Cape Breton when the French Revolution broke out. With Mi'kmaq Indian guides and a canoe, with simple surveying equipment, Crawley, sometimes assisted by Captain William Cox of present-day Coxheath, meticulously plotted the base lines for surveys, and planned land grant patterns throughout the island. Generally, the Scots lived on 200-acre grants for farming while the Acadians wanted six- or seven-acre grants along the water so that they could pursue the fishery. From almost fifty years of surveying the island, Thomas Crawley became the person most familiar with its peoples, its geography and its needs. An example of Crawley's importance can be seen in the fact that he was the only person who retained his appointment after Cape Breton was annexed to Nova Scotia in 1820. Every other officeholder was dismissed, but Crawley's knowledge of the island was of precious value to the Nova Scotia government, which was relatively ignorant of the geography and people of its new acquisition. The new government was determined to lay out land for the Indians in reservations; Crawley laid out the reservations at Whycocomagh [Waycobah], Middle River [Wagmatcook], and Eskasoni. When the government in Halifax sought information on the products of the island, Crawley supplied the information; it was he who laid out the boundaries of three of Cape Breton's four counties. His description of the settlements of the island and his recommendation for assistance to the settlers during the island's great famine of 1845-51 showed his deep interest in the development and welfare of Cape Breton. As demands grew for plans, descriptions, affidavits, and the preparation of grants of purchased lands, he employed a clerk out of his own pocket. In 1832 alone he was asked to compile a list of all land grants on Cape Breton. This required 7374 searches. He retired with a pension of £120 per year in addition to his naval superannuation, and at his death left a son who was a founder of the Arts department of Acadia University, another who became Commissionaire of Crown Lands for Cape Breton, and another, Edward, who founded Horton Academy and was the first president of Acadia University.

These four great pioneer surveyors—one French, one Dutch, one Swiss and one English—serve as shining beacons to the profession of surveying not only in Cape Breton but in the whole of Canada. To me, they show the great variety of personalities who are attracted to the profession, some phlegmatic, some flamboyant, others ambitious, others self-sacrificing. Yet it seems the common characteristics of these four surveyors, which typify the whole profession, are exactitude, imagination, physical fearlessness, artistry and just plain hard work, which have made the surveyor a much-admired figure. They are the first to go to uncharted lands; thanks to them, the rest of us can follow.

5

Ranna Cossit:
The Loyalist Rector
of St. George's Church

THE AUTUMN OF 1785 was ablaze in Cape Breton Island and in its little capital, Sydney. The town stood among the trees, hardly more than a clearing, on a peninsula jutting out into a magnificent harbour. The settlement had been founded just that spring by a group of Loyalists and British settlers. This was no ordinary settlement, however. Sydney was to be the capital of the new Colony of Cape Breton which, like New Brunswick, had been chosen as a home for the Loyalists forced from the rebellious colonies by the American Revolution.

The island was a wilderness. No appreciable settlement had taken place since the Fortress of Louisbourg had fallen to the British in 1758. After the dispersal of the French from the Fortress, the British had failed to develop the island. Louisbourg lay in ruins and outlying settlements like Spanish Bay, now Sydney, had been abandoned. Then, as a result of the American Revolution, thousands of Loyalists began moving northward. In the spring of 1785, DesBarres and his fellow settlers crossed Spanish Bay and founded Sydney as the Colony of Cape Breton's capital. During that summer, troops of the 33rd Regiment were sent from Halifax to garrison and help clear the land. More Loyalists also arrived and an air of optimism prevailed. The governor's house was erected, along with barracks, bakehouses and other public buildings.

This was the scene which greeted the new prospective minister when he first saw Sydney during the autumn of 1785. Ranna Cossit was greatly impressed with the prospects of the colony as well as its lieutenant-governor and the settlers. On their part, they seemed pleased with the young 41-year-old cleric with his dark curly hair, deep blue eyes and determined air.

Determination is one thing Ranna Cossit possessed in full measure. For generations his family had sought to lead their chosen way of life free from the tyranny of those who would impose their ideas on them. The name Cossit is of French origin; one René Cossett had emigrated from Paris to Trois Rivières, Quebec, as a young man, but around 1712, perhaps unhappy with life there, had migrated to Connecticut and anglicized his first son's name to Ranna and Cossett to Cossit.

The young man was intelligent and persistent so his father sent him off to the newly-formed Rhode Island College where he received his Bachelor of Arts degree in 1771. By that time, Ranna expressed an interest in studying for the priesthood, which meant that he had to study in England. After two years of intensive study he was ordained a priest of the Church of England by the Bishop of London on 7 March 1773.

On his return to America, the young man moved westward to the pioneer area of Claremont, New Hampshire, where he served as a missionary for the Society for the Propagation of the Gospel in Foreign Parts (SPG). His charge included an area that extended from Claremont to Haverhill, seventy miles to the north. This meant frequent journeys through semi-wilderness with all the attendant dangers, experiences that would be useful one day in Cape Breton.

But even greater challenges faced Cossit. New Hampshire was rife with dissatisfaction over its links with Great Britain. Cossit had become more and more aware of this, but perhaps because he studied in London, he favoured conciliation and retention of the ancient ties with Britain. The very fact that he returned to the Colonies, and indeed to the backwoods where rebel sentiment was strong, indicated Cossit's fearless sense of determination to support any cause in which he believed. Incapable of doing anything by halfway measures, he stoutly defended the cause of King and Country.

As the clouds of revolution gathered, one bright spot appeared in Cossit's life, for he fell in love with and married eighteen-year-old Thankfull Brooks, one of his parishioners, in June 1774. Thankfull's life was slated to be one of unrelenting hardship.

Far from the centre of law and order, Cossit was open to personal attack from the rebellious backwoodsmen. Six months after his marriage, a mob of 300 men threatened his life. Now he had to think of his wife, who was pregnant and would bear him a son in August. The Claremont rebels organized a Joint Committee of Safety to root out Loyalists who disagreed with their course of action. To Cossit they represented the end of civilized government and he was determined to resist.

Consequently, in the following December he and around twenty other Anglicans were arrested and brought before the Committee of Safety. Upon examination Cossit firmly proclaimed his loyalty and added: "I believe the American Colonies in their dispute with Great Britain...are unjust...I verily believe the British troops will overcome by the greatness of their power and the justice of their cause."[1]

Cossit's open defiance, so typical of the man, earned him confinement within the town limits of Claremont, without weapons to defend himself. He continued his clerical duties, openly offering up prayers for the King. This brought further persecution upon him and his fellow Loyalists: they were confined in jails, beaten, and drawn through mud and water. All during the winter and spring of 1776 Cossit was cross-

examined for his beliefs, but to no avail, for that May he refused to sign the so-called Declaration of Independence by the
People of New Hampshire.

With continued persecution, his fellow Loyalists gradually left the region. "In sundry places," Cossit wrote, "where I
used to officiate, the Church people are all dwindled away.
Some have fled to the King's army for protection, some were
banished, and many died."[2] Many moved northward to Canada but their determined minister stayed, sending information
to the British north of the border, and indeed visiting Quebec
in November 1782 to bring information concerning the
events in his area. During this time, Abraham Cuyler, the
mayor of Albany, New York, who would one day move to
Cape Breton, became familiar with Cossit's work and
personality.

In 1783 Britain signed the Treaty of Versailles recogniz-
ing the independence of thirteen of her former colonies. Although Loyalist refugees were streaming northward, Cossit
still stubbornly remained convinced that at least northern
New Hampshire and Vermont might be brought back to British rule. By then as the only Anglican priest in New Hampshire, he had a great many more services to perform. After the
Revolution, the SPG was forbidden to employ missionaries in
the United States, though former missionaries continued to
receive allowances until Michaelmas 1785. To add to these
problems, his family was increasing in size. Between January
1777 and April 1785, Thankfull bore him three more sons
and three daughters. One of the boys died, leaving him to provide for six children and a wife. Faced with a dwindling congregation but a growing family, with continued distrust by the
surrounding population and fearing the end of his allowance
from the SPG, even Cossit was forced to give in and seek a
new mission.[3]

There was no shortage of positions, since new parishes

were springing up in the newly-settled loyal colonies to the north. On 29 April 1785, the Rev. William Morice, secretary of the SPG, wrote offering Cossit a post in Cape Breton which would bring £120 annually. This offer included a house and glebe lands, and even financial help in moving his family and household. To the Cossit family this seemed like a miracle, as Ranna's allowance from the SPG for his work in New Hampshire was due to expire and his young family was facing destitution.

By the fall, Cossit, who had made the long trip to Cape Breton, was standing aboard a ship sailing into Spanish Bay. Within a few hours he was in the forest clearing called Sydney and talking to Lieutenant-Governor DesBarres. DesBarres agreed to the terms of Cossit's appointment, and since the minister was also in charge of education in the colony, a temporary schoolhouse-church was promised, together with a parsonage. With a promise to return the following spring, Cossit sailed for Boston to gather supplies and make a final plea for his loyal churchmen from New Hampshire among whom he would truly have loved to have settled in the Eastern Townships of Quebec. This would never be, and though Cossit's future seemed assured, the poignant separation from his beloved countrymen was a tragedy faced by all Loyalists. It was a trial he would encounter again one day.

Now, however, Cossit had to start his new life on the northern cape. He decided to leave his wife and children with Thankfull's family and friends, and returned to Sydney in the spring of 1786. Disappointment faced him there. The building intended as a temporary church and school had been blown down in a gale, his rectory had not yet been begun, and he was informed that the British government would not supply money for the church until it was completed. It was like starting again at Claremont thirteen years earlier.

His first duty was to his family, and he built a house on

Charlotte Street, located midway between the governor's house and the site chosen for the new parish church. The two-story house with six fireplaces was a fair-sized one for the little colony, but Cossit would need space for his growing family. Since there was no sawmill yet erected, it appears Cossit used lumber previously cut and imported, perhaps first used in the construction of the schoolhouse-church which had blown down. The broad arrow, the mark of government property, carved into the beams of the roof of the house, indicated that it had had previous use. One story of old Sydney is that the wood came from Virginia. It is possible that the wood, imported in the early days of the colony before a sawmill was erected, came from many distant locations.

While he had luck with his house, which was ready by early 1787, the erection of a church was more difficult. In October 1786, the first two church wardens were elected and Cossit, with the co-operation of DesBarres, laid the foundation of a stone church at the head of Nepean Street, overlooking Sydney Harbour.

The colony, however, was poor, and the provision that money would not be forthcoming from London until the church was completed slowed progress even more. Material had to be acquired as cheaply as possible; some of the stone for the walls of the church was taken from the abandoned Fortress of Louisbourg. By Christmas Day 1789, Cossit held the first church service in the new church, christened St. George's. Even though there were no pews, pulpit or seats, another step forward had been taken in the little colony.

As soon as the parsonage was habitable, while St. George's was still under construction, Cossit returned to Claremont to collect his family. He probably spent the winter of 1788 there, settling his affairs and bidding farewell to his friends. In the spring he was back in Sydney, which was becoming home.

But Sydney was entering a difficult period.[4] The Colony of Cape Breton had been separated from the jurisdiction of Nova Scotia in 1784, almost as an afterthought, in order to accommodate an expected influx of Loyalists. This division however had been made too late, since Loyalists had already settled in mainland Nova Scotia and New Brunswick in 1783, two years before Sydney was founded. They preferred locating in the more established colony of Nova Scotia or in New Brunswick which was closer to their former homes. Cape Breton was still a wilderness, unattractive to new settlers seeking at least some of the amenities of civilized life. As late as 1790 there was no doctor, no teacher, and before Cossit, no minister in the Colony. When Abraham Cuyler had sought to settle the island, he promised to bring 3,000 Loyalists. Instead, he brought fewer than 150. Although new Loyalists continued to move in until around 1790 from almost all the former colonies, previous settlers emigrated just as quickly. Consequently Sydney grew slowly. In 1795 there were only 121 people living there, 26 of whom were preparing to leave. Houses which had gone up with such promise in 1785 were abandoned; 27 homes lay in ruins.

This problem would be readily understandable if Cape Breton were resourceless. Instead, the island had an abundance of natural resources such as coal, timber, fish and gypsum. But these resources, particularly coal, needed capital for full development. Britain, fearing competition at home from this coal or from industries which might locate near mines, was in no hurry to see the mines flourish, and capital was subsequently not forthcoming. The other three resources were still in their infancy and their development did not begin until after the turn of the century.

The management of the mines passed from one lessee to another. In most cases the operators had no mining experience and very little capital. Sydney, which should have been a wealthy industrial centre, languished in its early days.

The main revenue in the tiny capital was money spent by the garrison and officials, largely on rum. If these few officials and merchants could have been taxed, at least their money could have been spent on colonial improvements. Taxation, however, was forbidden. This may have been the Colonial Office's way of attracting settlers or of insuring that new people would not be exploited, but it meant that the lieutenant-governor and his Council were impotent in trying to build roads or public buildings.

Therefore, the early years of the colony tell a story of frustration. Loyalists like Abraham Cuyler or David Mathews, who had come to Cape Breton hoping to regain some of the losses they had sustained in the American Revolution, were disappointed in the colony's prospects. They were appointed to high office. Cuyler for example was secretary and registrar of the colony; Mathews was attorney-general; both were on the Executive Council. However, they could hardly use their office to advance their wealth, since the colony was poverty-stricken. This simply angered them, and they blamed lieutenant-governors like DesBarres. DesBarres on the other hand was a strong-willed man with military training who was opposed to privilege and determined to be sole ruler of the colony.

The inevitable clashes between the lieutenant-governors and members of the Executive Council may have been settled had a house of assembly been established. Instead, the Colonial Office had decided that no house of assembly would be elected until the island's population warranted it. Superficially, this seems reasonable. In reality, it had the effect of keeping settlers away, which in return delayed the granting of an assembly. The meetings of the lieutenant-governor with his executive thus became forums of debate. This delayed decisions and prevented action from being taken to cure the colony's ills. Cuyler and Mathews succeeded in convincing the Colonial Office that DesBarres was a tyrant and unfit to rule. He was recalled and replaced by Lieutenant-Governor William Macarmick in 1787.

The struggle to remove DesBarres had not been a complete victory for the powerful Loyalists. Some members of the Executive Council, and many people, both Loyalist and otherwise, supported DesBarres. A rift developed which led to two factions, which persisted throughout the life of the colony. The varying success of each side makes up a large part of the political history of Cape Breton until 1820.

Cossit tried to avoid these intrigues. In June 1786 he wrote, "Seeing I could do no good in these matters, I avoided as much as I conveniently could, anything, as I am determined, as much as in me lieth, to live peaceably with all men...."[5] Possibly his mind was on his own responsibilities as another daughter was born in 1789 and another son two years later. With more mouths to feed, finances became more important, particularly when his salary from the SPG was delayed. However, Cossit complained very little about this slowness, but busied himself with his clerical duties. He hired the colony's first teacher, Hiram Payne, in 1790, and classes were taught in the parsonage. He managed to obtain £500 from the British government for the completion of St. George's Church in 1791. Meanwhile his missionary duties continued. They must have reminded him of the early days in Claremont, except that the territory was broader and communications even more primitive. He made trips by horseback to Main-à-Dieu, Louisbourg and Cow Bay [Port Morien]. The dangers of such expeditions are exemplified in this story told by Cossit's great-great-grandson:

"Rev. Ranna, on one occasion was returning from a visit to Cow Bay, and nightfall found him at the Inn at Hines Road. He left his horse with a stable hand to be fed and wa-

tered and went into the Inn for his supper. During the course
of his meal he noticed two very unsavory characters in a corner
of the room. They were talking in whispers, glancing in his di-
rection, and soon left the room. Rev. Ranna suspected they
were up to no good. When he finished his meal and paid the
host, he went outside where he found his horse, fed and saddled. Mounting, he kept a wary eye on the shadows and before
long he saw the two outlaws jump from the bushes and seize
his bridle. Slipping the sword from its sheath, he caught one of
the men across the face and swinging on the other, cut the arm
holding the horse. Spurring his mount, he then left the cul-
prits who were howling in pain and rode off. Needless to say,
he was not molested after this."[6]

Cossit's reaction offers another insight into the determined spirit of the Cape Breton rector. Such a man would not
bow to enemies of what he considered the cause of Cape Breton, and it was not long before Cossit became involved in the
colony's politics. He distrusted Cuyler and Mathews in their
opposition to the established authority of the lieutenant-
governor. Though he was a democrat, Cossit would not toler-
ate what he saw as a return to the unruly situation which had
led to revolution in New Hampshire.

At first he was too busy organizing his parish and family
to participate in politics. He observed however that:

"Discontent, Envy and Malice are much more dominant
here than true Religion on account of contention of some
principal men (having commissions both Civil and Military)
with the governor to the great prejudice of the settlement.
These contentions, with many false reports against the governor, have kept many industrious farmers and fishermen...from becoming settlers on this Island, when they had
made all preparations for so doing in order to enjoy the British
Constitution which they esteem to be the Wisdom of God
and the Glory of the whole Earth."[7]

Cossit firmly believed that the protection of the British Constitution was the duty of the established church; it was therefore only a matter of time before he, as that church's minister, became involved in the political life of the colony. This was hastened by his appointment to the Executive Council, which brought him in close proximity to Mathews and Cuyler. By the time Cossit became actively involved in politics, Cuyler had left the colony. Lieutenant-Governor Macarmick relaxed for a while, but asked to be removed in 1795. As senior member of Council, David Mathews was appointed administrator until a replacement could be found for Macarmick.

Cossit had established himself as the chief enemy of Mathews when the latter tried to form a group to prevent the settlement of Acadians in Cape Breton. Cossit alleged that Mathews' group would "subvert the good order of Society."[8] Macarmick agreed and squelched Mathews' alliance, thus allowing the free settlement of Acadians in Isle Madame. After this incident, Macarmick kept a close eye on Mathews, but on Macarmick's departure, Mathews took out his enmity on Cossit and his followers. Cossit's chief ally was James Miller, a mineralogist sent by the Colonial Office to investigate and make recommendations on the operations of the coal mines. Miller condemned the haphazard mining methods followed by the private individuals, Richard Stout and John Tremaine, to whom the mines had been leased. Stout was the colony's principal merchant and Mathews was in debt to him. Miller's call for public ownership endangered Stout's position and caused Mathews to unleash an unrelenting attack on him.

Cossit and Miller were natural allies, not only in their distrust of Mathews, but also in condemning the overuse of rum in payment to miners. The miners lived gloomy lives punctuated by drunken revelries, during one of which their barracks burned to the ground. Cossit could not countenance this and with Miller argued that the miners should be paid in cash. Mathews not only supported Stout, but also failed to attend church. This alienated Cossit, so when Mathews allowed his name to stand for vestryman, the rector was furious and he and his followers succeeded in preventing the election.

Mathews' revenge came quickly. When in the fall of 1795 Cossit as SPG agent attempted to appoint a new teacher, Mathews and his followers appointed their own, thus diminishing any tuition Cossit's choice might gain. Cossit opened the school at his home, so Mathews had the schoolmaster arrested for debt, but Cossit and Miller gave security for the schoolmaster.

As others became involved in these and other quarrels, the Colonial Office took action to remove Mathews. Two administrators followed: Major General James Ogilvie, the former commander-in-chief of troops in the Maritime region, and Brigadier-General John Murray. Before Ogilvie arrived, Mathews managed to have Cossit imprisoned for a £25 debt which the latter allegedly owed Mathews' son. Ogilvie released Cossit, blaming Mathews for the factionalism, and Murray, who succeeded Ogilvie after less than a year, agreed. Cossit and his allies accordingly emerged triumphant in 1799.

The victory lasted less than a year, as Murray's successor, General John Despard, arrived to replace him in June 1800. Murray felt he was being unduly replaced and fought to remain in Sydney. While the decision of Whitehall was being awaited, Cossit and his followers rallied behind Murray; Mathews supported Despard. When word arrived that Murray was to be replaced, Mathews emerged triumphant. The gain was also short-lived, however, since Mathews died before the year was out.

Despard now saw Cossit not only as a political enemy but also as a clergyman who had become too involved in politics and who had to be removed for the sake of colonial harmony.

Despard wrote asking that Bishop Charles Inglis give the rector a new parish.

Cossit, who had come to love Cape Breton, refused to leave. His oldest boy, also called Ranna, was already in his late twenties and taking a role in colonial politics. Although some of the older children were married, by 1802 Thankfull had given birth to two more children, giving a total family of thirteen, ten of whom survived. It would normally be difficult to provide for such a large family, but in the poor little colony it was a trial. At times it was hard to keep the children in shoes and, had the potato patch in the yard of the parsonage not been productive, it would have been difficult to keep all the mouths fed. The demands of birth and inadequate diet led to the greatest tragedy of Cossit's life: the death of Thankfull in childbirth at the age of 46. Her previous child had been delivered five years before, and the late pregnancy must have come as a surprise to the couple. Their joy ended in tragedy and the grief-stricken rector wrote poignantly in the parish register: "October 20th, 1802. Buried Mrs. Thankfull Cossit aged 46 years the 15th of March last—her whole life was ornamental to Christianity as a Wife, a Parent, a Neighbour...."[9]

The burial of his wife in Cape Breton soil, and his children's setting down roots in Sydney, were reasons enough for Cossit's desire to remain, but the increasing prosperity of the colony appeared to be a reward for all the hard work of fifteen years. In 1802 the first Scots began arriving from Scotland and, though poor, they began farming, fishing and shipbuilding. This had an immediate positive effect on the economy of the Colonial capital. Moreover, John Despard proved to be an outstanding administrator and soon increased the productivity of the mines and the extent of the colonial revenue.

But Cossit was not to enjoy his family or the brighter economy. Bishop Inglis himself arrived in Sydney in July 1805, and after three days convinced Cossit that his political involvement had caused scandal which could only hurt the Church. The sixty-one-year-old rector sadly agreed to leave all behind and accept an appointment far from his home in the remote town of Yarmouth.

The responsibilities at Yarmouth were onerous. As new rector, Cossit was charged with organizing the parish and building a church. The first site was abandoned due to wet ground. A second site was selected and the church was erected in July 1807. As in New Hampshire and Cape Breton, the aging man had to minister not only to the centre of population at Yarmouth, but also to Chebogue, Plymouth and Tusket. At first he pleaded to return to Sydney, but soon accepted his charge. He remained out of politics, perhaps because the capital of this colony lay 300 miles away, and served the growing parish at Yarmouth until his death 13 March 1815.

Ranna Cossit was a man of principle who acted for what he believed. These beliefs were simple: the advancement of the Kingdom of God on earth, and the righteousness of the British constitution as the instrument of that Kingdom. Any person who opposed these causes was his enemy, and he would fight them with all his strength.

Unlike most people, Cossit left behind tangible symbols of these beliefs: churches in Claremont, Sydney and Yarmouth mark his accomplishments. A cairn near Holy Trinity Church in Yarmouth proclaims his work there. His descendants are scattered all over North America in every walk of life.

On any summer day, the traveller to Sydney is able to visit a humble house on Charlotte Street. It is Ranna Cossit's own home, open to the public by the Nova Scotia Museum since 1977. It endures as the oldest standing home in Sydney, as a monument to the lasting qualities of the Loyalist rector and his wife, and as a reminder of the society they and other Loyalists fought to establish.

6

On the 195th Anniversary of
the Foundation of
St. George's Church

A TALK

SOME INSTITUTIONS faithfully reflect the life of their community. They rise, flourish, decline and grow with the settlement around them. They become identified with the community, become loved by it, so that citizens cannot imagine their city without it.

In Sydney, St. George's Church is such an institution. It witnessed Governor DesBarres and David Tait laying out the streets of the new capital of Cape Breton in the spring of 1785; when in 1788 the British Parliament voted £500 for setting up the church and parish of St. George's, the mines were just opening across the harbour. Ranna Cossit, whose name is now a household word in Sydney, was making priestly visits to the mines twice a month in 1796, six years before the great Scottish migration to Cape Breton began.

The first bishop to visit St. George's was Charles Inglis, who arrived in 1805, shortly after Governor Despard initiated the first tax in Cape Breton—this one was on rum. In 1819 the rector, Hibbert Binney, was looking for a steeple for the church since the parish clerk had donated a bell (and just as important, I might add, two stoves). A few days after that, making a clerical circuit, Mr. Binney rowed seven miles to Sydney Forks, then walked the six miles to the Portage where he hired an open sailboat. The next day he arrived at St. Pe-

71

ters, then moved on to Arichat in a birchbark canoe. On his return to Sydney he went to Mira, Louisbourg and Gabarus, officiating once or twice each day. Gabarus had never been visited by a minister of any religion. He baptized 62 people there. After leaving Louisbourg, Binney decided to return to Sydney by horse on the newly-constructed Louisbourg road. His horse broke through a bridge and the poor man had to continue by foot to the capital city.

A year after this trip, Cape Breton was annexed to Nova Scotia, but St. George's was still the parish church of Cape Breton Island, and the only church in the old capital city.

Strangely enough, St. George's was not consecrated until 1833, after it had been in continuous use for over fifty-five years. What was the Sydney of the 1830s like? It was, plainly speaking, a cow town, since cows literally roamed the streets freely. Horses' harnesses were made of straw and one man, Robert Martin, Sydney's fourth postmaster, could remember a cow eating the harness off a horse in Sydney. By the way, horses used to bring the produce in from the country not by cart but on drags—a pair of poles, one hung each side of the horse and the other end trailing on the ground. People would leave the poles in town for firewood and ride home on horseback. At that time (the 1830s) there wasn't a cart to be seen between Sydney Forks and St. Peters, except one owned by a man named Howie.

The army or garrison used St. George's and lived at present Victoria Park. The money they spent was an important part of the economy of the old capital city.

In the 1840s the mail was delivered once a week. Only one block from St. George's, where the masonic building is now located [Esplanade near Dorchester Street], was a bog with a cattle path through it. The only churches were St. George's [on Charlotte Street] and St. Patrick's [on the Esplanade]. People in those days could remember getting lost in the woods where the post office is located [corner of Dorchester and Charlotte Streets, at the time of this talk], and that the area was a great hunting ground for moose and caribou.

Most of the town's leading citizens, those who laid the foundations of Sydney, attended St. George's. Edmund Murray Dodd, M.L.A., a committed separatist who could not believe Cape Breton should have been annexed to Nova Scotia, lies buried in St. George's cemetery. There was H. W. Crawley, commissioner of Crown Lands, who owned most of the land along Charlotte Street between Dorchester and Pitt Streets, and whose name is remembered at Crawley's Creek; Charles R. Ward, high sheriff and editor of the *Cape Bretonian*, the island's first regular newspaper; Peter Hall Clark, ancestor of the Clarks of Sydney; Charles Dumeresq, architect; Richard Gibbons, barrister; William Bown, Thomas Jost, James Anderson and Thomas Rigby, merchants; John LeCras, blacksmith; Christopher Welton, shoemaker; Charles E. Leonard, collector of customs. All of the names ring faint bells in our minds—they are remembered perhaps by a street name, perhaps by a building or a story, or a tombstone. But their lives went into the fabric of the old capital. St. George's nourished these people and became part of this contribution.

But time does not stop. The church needed repairs and the central tower was replaced by a wooden steeple at the west end of the church. In 1852 the Rt. Reverend Hibbert Binney, son of the fourth rector of St. George's (already mentioned), visited as a son returning home. It was a moment of pride for Sydney, and the old capital certainly had pride.

Many visitors remarked that although Sydney had lost her capital city status with Cape Breton's annexation to Nova Scotia in 1820, she behaved as if nothing had happened. Lieutenant B. W. A. Sleigh visited Sydney around that time. He described how the garrison marched to St. George's. He described the congregation as, "a vista of young and elderly ladies, very flashily dressed, with airs of considerable pride and conceit."

He added: "A long, uninteresting sermon, urgently recommending subscriptions for some mission to Timbuctoo or other African locality, formed the theme of the clergyman's discourse. The Military pew, which was close to the altar, had an uninterrupted view through a door, which was open, over a fine expanse of well-wooded luxuriant country...."

Sleigh, however, was generally fond of the old capital. He delighted in the "refined tone of conversation" which was to be found here and found that "our time was plesantly diversified." He claimed he never heard a military man who had been stationed in Cape Breton who had not spoken of the hospitality of the people.

However, the people were not saints. Duelling was a frequent means of settling arguments. Richard Gibbons—the Great Separatist, the irascible attorney-general before annexation, the cranky lawyer who was once called the "Robespierre of Cape Breton"—once fought a duel with Mr. Pooley, the schoolmaster. Gibbons was hit in the hip and could never ride horseback again.

Two crises struck St. George's in the 1850s and 1860s. First, in 1854, the garrison was withdrawn from Sydney to fight in the Crimea. One can imagine the broken hearts of the town belles left behind. The economy of the town also suffered, since the military played a role proportional to that which it plays in Halifax today. Henceforth, St. George's depended on its own people for support.

Secondly, in the 1860s, the rector, Reverend Richard John Uniacke, decided to have work done on the walls of the church. The result was that they collapsed, necessitating an almost complete rebuilding of the edifice.

Both the old capital and the church survived these blows, and by the 1870s prosperity was beginning to appear as coal mines began to serve the towns growing up around them. The Great Gale of August 1873 destroyed the church tower, but a few years later a new tower replaced it.

The town and parish had come a long way together by 1885, when Sydney celebrated its centennial. One man recorded his thoughts in that year:

"One hundred years, of course, has wrought many changes in Sydney, but the town is still small for its age. It has, however, expanded fairly well within its conditions. 1886 will be its initial year under incorporation, and much may be expected from the wisdom of the councillors. The prosperity of the place depends almost entirely upon the development of the mineral resources of the island. The man who writes up the next centennial will certainly have many improvements to notice, and I hope that he may be able to say, 'Lo, here lies the Canadian Birmingham.'"

St. George's celebrated with a window dedicated to Sir John Bourinot, a native son who wrote the rules of Parliament for Canada and the Empire.

Since 1886, the city has undergone many changes. With development of DOSCO and DISCO [Dominion Steel and Coal Corporation, and Dominion Iron and Steel Company], the old capital appeared to be heading toward becoming Canada's Birmingham. In 1904 the town became a city. St. George's witnessed this and saw the city expand away from the old North End and toward Ashby, Whitney Pier and the Shipyard. She seemed like a queen whose new subjects had all moved away. She was left among the buildings of the old capital with her back to the steel plant. Early in this century her little tower and graveyard looked forlorn and alone.

Yet the isolation of the North End has been a blessing, since a new generation, one that is preparing to celebrate the two hundredth anniversary of the founding of Sydney, looks not only ahead, but is seeking to preserve the heritage of which

St. George's is a vital part. That area of Sydney between St. George's Church and DesBarres Street, between the Esplanade and the west side of George Street, is one of the best preserved historical neighbourhoods of Atlantic Canada. In most places, such areas have long since been replaced by new buildings. In Sydney, all the growth occurred to the south of the centre of the old town.

Hence Old Sydney still lives in the North End. In this area we have eighteenth- and nineteenth-century buildings of every style. Cossit House, Sydney's first private residence, is a fine example of simple eighteenth-century elegance. It and the house next door, which was built in 1790, take us back to Sydney's days as a colonial capital. The gables on the house next to the Cossit House were added in the 1850s when the neo-Gothic style found favour in the old capital. This was a time of growing prosperity in Sydney. Down the street is an old courthouse dating from 1832, with the cells still extant in the basement. Nearby is the house where Irish prisoners were kept in the cellar in 1788; further down is the house whose frame is partly composed of the scaffolding used to hang the perpetrators of Sydney's first important murder in 1833. Then there is St. Patrick's Church, built in 1828 and eastern Nova Scotia's oldest standing Roman Catholic church. We have Victorian mansions, flat-roofed houses of the eighteenth century, neo-classical houses of the 1840s. All of this is within a relatively small, beautiful area. They are led by their oldest building, St. George's, which has been there for 195 years.

As Sydney and St. George's approach their 200th anniversary together [1985], it is incumbent on all of us, from the mayor down to the youngest citizen, to do all we can to preserve our heritage. Now is the time to begin planning for the bicentennial of the old capital. Not only should celebrations be held, fine speeches made, beautiful parades staged, but something of lasting value should be left behind. Hopefully, within the next year, the province's long-awaited heritage legislation will be passed. This will permit, with government assistance, the preservation of whole historical neighbourhoods. You can see how this will apply to Sydney. All we need is the support of the City Fathers. The time of uphill battles, such as ones the Old Sydney Society has fought for the past several years, should be over. City Council should not need to be lobbied; they should suggest the preservation of the area around St. George's. This would be a suitable bicentennial project. If they need convincing, they should know that last year alone over 10,000 people visited the three historic buildings—St. George's, Cossit House and the Old Sydney Museum—which are open to the public in the North End. These tourists left money and spread the word that Sydney's reputation as a dirty steel town was untrue. They took the message that the old capital is a fascinating city with an interesting history.

St. George's is, partially at least, a monument—a monument to the development of our city. It should remind us that we owe something to those who came before us—we owe them honour and remembrance. It can also be a message to the future, not so much like the man 100 years ago who wanted us to become a Canadian Birmingham, but a message that we cared enough to pass on to the future what we inherited from the past. In this way, our Cape Breton culture and heritage will be kept. Our uniqueness will be preserved and the man who writes 100 years hence will say: "Lo! They preserved their heritage and passed on to us our identity."

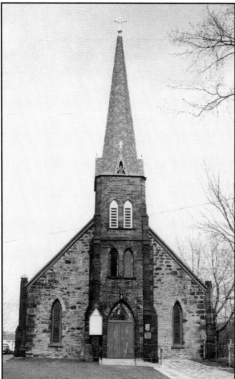

The Great Seal of the Colony of Cape Breton, George III. The motto FORTUNA NON MUTAT GENUS means, roughly, "Fortune (circumstance) does not change the race."

Top: St. George's Anglican Church, Nepean and Charlotte Streets; Cossit House: the home of Rev. Ranna Cossit, Charlotte Street; left: St. Patrick's Catholic Church (until 1950) now St. Patrick's Museum, Esplanade—all in Sydney's North End. *Courtesy the Beaton Institute, UCCB.*

7

Cape Breton's Debt to John Despard

IN THE TOWN OF OSWESTRY, England, not far from the Welsh border, stands the pre-Norman Church of St. Oswald's. A celtic cross rises among the rhododendrons growing in the churchyard; nearby, the close-cropped lawn with its well-kept tombstones contrasts sharply with the rear of the churchyard, where a tangle of holly, ivy and leeks covers the graves of the forgotten. It is in this unkempt section that General John Despard, Cape Breton's most able administrator, lies buried.

When he arrived in Sydney in 1801, Despard found a poor, bickering colony with its population declining and its mines in trouble; in 1807, he left behind a growing colony with bright prospects. He managed Cape Breton honestly and faithfully, despite an illness which was described as "a most violent fit of gout or cramps in the stomach,"[1] probably bleeding ulcers, which finally killed him in 1829 at the age of 83.

Despard already had a long military career behind him when he arrived in Sydney; he had fought in twenty-four engagements, had two horses shot from under him, and had three times been shipwrecked. He had fought the Americans at Quebec in 1775, and in Virginia and Charleston, South Carolina. He returned to England after the American Revolution, but was again stationed in Quebec in 1793, and Halifax in 1795.[2] In 1800, Colonel Despard was appointed administrator of Cape Breton.

Cape Breton was a challenge. In 1784 she had been politically separated from Nova Scotia. Lieutenant-Governor Joseph F. W. DesBarres left in 1787 angry and bitter at the Colonial Office and at the Loyalist leaders, David Mathews[3] and Abraham Cuyler,[4] both of whom despised DesBarres's dictatorial habits. DesBarres had a great deal of power. But with no house of assembly to stop them, his Executive Council—much like modern City Councils except that they were not elected—vied with him for power and fought him continually.

DesBarres' replacement, William Macarmick, despite his good intentions, fell into this habit of quarreling with Mathews and Cuyler. Macarmick witnessed the decline of Sydney's population to 121, then to 95, all cloistered at the north end of town. The mines were not producing enough coal, and a new level had to be dug at Indian Cove; meanwhile, troops which supplied the liquor trade—the Sydney merchants' chief form of livelihood—had been largely withdrawn.

Macarmick, however, was not alone in his battles with members of the Executive Council, for within the Council itself another group or "party" developed who opposed Mathews and Cuyler and who were led by the irrepressible Reverend Ranna Cossit, rector of St. George's Church. Cossit and his followers managed to gain Macarmick's support by 1795 and dominated the Executive Council despite Mathews' and Cuyler's protests.

This situation did not last long, for in 1795 Macarmick decided to return to Great Britain to rejoin his wife who had been captured in France during the French Revolution. He left David Mathews as senior councillor in charge of Cape Breton until his replacement should arrive. Mathews took his vengeance; within two years Cossit and many of his supporters, including Ingram Ball, found themselves in the DesBarres Street jail.[5] Though they were eventually released, the struggle for power continued between Cossit and his supporters, and when Mathews died in 1800, his successor as senior councillor was Archibald Charles Dodd, who lies buried in St. George's graveyard. Dodd was an Englishman and despised Cossit, the New Hampshire Loyalist. Dodd hated the Scot William McKinnon, one of Cossit's followers, even more.[6] At a vestry meeting at St. George's, McKinnon challenged Dodd to a duel on the grounds that Dodd had called Mrs. McKinnon a liar.[7] The duel was averted, probably by the Reverend Cossit.

Sydney's political situation was shocking to all the other Maritime capitals. Selfish parties grasping for power were the talk not only of Charlotte and York Streets, but of Halifax, which was always anxious to annex Cape Breton to Nova Scotia.

Despard inherited this situation. The Sydney he found was a strange colonial capital. Despite DesBarres's great plans, it had not developed—the Esplanade, Charlotte Street and Great George Street were the only north-south streets cleared of stumps. Charlotte veered toward George near the present Falmouth Street, and together they formed a path leading toward the Mira River, where winter waterfowl were caught. Cross streets included DesBarres, Amelia, York, and Dorchester. They ran from the harbour only to George Street.

On the other side of Great George Street was swampy land already fancifully called the Louisa Gardens, perhaps after one of DesBarres's daughters. St. George's was standing—but had no pews or pulpit, and certainly no bell or even steeple. A. C. Dodd lived near where the Royal Bank once stood, and Cossit's house still stands on Charlotte Street. The governor lived about 250 feet back from DesBarres Street, between Charlotte and present Campbell Street, in a drafty government house that had to double as a courthouse and meeting place for the Executive Council.

The troops lived at the barracks at Victoria Park. People

of quality lived at Point Edward, near Crawley's Creek, or Point Amelia.

And outside of Sydney? A few scattered farms. The Loyalist Captain Cox was already growing his famous strawberries at his farm in Cox's Heath, and Ingram Ball, previously co-chief justice of Cape Breton, lived with his large family at the creek which bears his name. The Rudderhams lived at the lime kiln on the west side of Point Edward; John Rudderham was one of the colony's best carpenters, as was his friend John Muggah who also did a bit of shipping on the side.

Beyond this was forest. To the south was Louisbourg, a shrunken Louisbourg with few families; only four decent homes stood there, and French cannons rotted on the harbour's shore, while the ribs of French ships still protruded from the water.[8] The Lorways, Skinners, Kennedys and Tutties must have faced cold damp winters in the foggy ghost town. Two prominent inhabitants had deserted Louisbourg as early as 1780. Charles Martell, who had lived near the ruins of the old French hospital in block 20, had moved to Main-à-Dieu, where he was appointed justice of the peace by 1787. Lawrence Kavanagh moved to St. Peters where he was a merchant among the 600 or so French, Acadians and a few Irish in the region. Nearby, Arichat was by far Cape Breton's largest town with around 200 people. They were mainly fishermen whose catch went to Spain, Jersey, Barbados or even Majorca. They brought home most of the foreign imports Cape Breton Island received, including the black rum which is still a characteristic drink among Cape Bretoners. Apart from shipping, there was very little contact between Sydney and Arichat.

Beyond this Acadian area was more forest. The Bras d'Or Lakes shore was virtually uninhabited except at Baddeck, where Jonathan Jones and twenty or thirty Loyalists were farming near Baddeck River. In the present Port Hood area lived the Smiths—descendants of the Loyalist David Smith;

they inhabited the present Port Hood Island which, in 1800, was still part of the Cape Breton mainland.

Judique held a few Scottish squatters who could not get land in Prince Edward Island. Beyond this, there was Cheticamp, where about 100 people, refugees from St. Pierre and Miquelon when the French Revolution erupted, fished for the Robin Company, a Jersey firm located also in Arichat as well as in New Brunswick. The Robin Company was the island's major employer. Ingonish alone was left; hay was grown there to feed the horses used in the mines.

The only other inhabitants of Cape Breton were the Mi'kmaq Indians who hunted and gathered berries; around 450 of them lived on Cape Breton around 1800; of this number, 130 were able hunters who used the bow and arrow, but who could also hurl their tomahawks with precision eight to ten yards. All were Roman Catholics, converted by the French before the fall of Louisbourg.

Altogether the colony held no more than 2,500 people who were mainly poor and illiterate. Roads were non-existent, the mines in a mess. Sydney, the capital, was in decline and out of touch with the rest of the colony, bickering over politics, while houses, as quickly as they were deserted, were used as firewood by their neighbours. Indeed, Cape Breton had more moose than people; in 1787, more than 11,000 were killed by Yankee smugglers, and in 1805, A. C. Dodd reported sighting 1,500 caribou on the Gabarus barrens between Louisbourg and Gabarus.

John Despard arrived in this stagnant little orphan colony 16 June 1800, with his wife Harriet Ann and daughter Elizabeth, together with his nephew William, who served as his private secretary, and his nephew's wife. Government House must have brightened up considerably after the bachelor days of the preceding administrators.

Initially, Despard had to settle the mines problem. First

he leased them to the colony's attorney-general, Alexander Campbell. Campbell, however, could not operate them properly.[9] Consequently Despard took over the mines in the name of the Crown; immediately they began to produce. He hired the most capable John Ritchie, a Halifax merchant, and ancestor of the Sydney Ritchies, as mines' superintendent. Mine production increased to near 7,000 chaldrons (38,000 bushels) per year.[10] Meanwhile, the mines' level was extended, a new pit was completed, and the wharf at the mines strengthened and extended to deeper water so that larger ships could be easily loaded.[11] Sydney could now supply Halifax and Newfoundland with adequate amounts of coal, and more money began to flow into the colony.

Meanwhile, Despard turned his attention to the land situation. Like everything else, it was in confusion. When DesBarres arrived in 1785, he made free land grants to Loyalists; non-Loyalists who could not afford land were given leases which expired at the lessee's death. Macarmick wanted to make all land holdings permanent, but in 1789, London decreed that no more land grants were to be made in Cape Breton. One purpose for this policy was to obtain money to maintain the colonial establishment; Pitt had decided that this policy would cause land values to rise, bringing more money into the hands of the government. Unfortunately, this policy proved disastrous, and only kept settlers from Cape Breton. Most settlers had to be content with leases, and many decided simply to squat without paying any money.

Despard was not discouraged by such a situation; he quickly noticed that a good deal of the land granted by DesBarres had never been improved or settled. Land, particularly 100,000 acres around the Mira River, had been granted and only a few settlers, among them David Tait, a Florida Loyalist who with DesBarres had first planned out Sydney's streets, had even settled there. So Despard set up an escheats court which was empowered to take over land from those who had never settled there.[12] Hence thousands of acres of land in Cape Breton became available by 1802, just at a time when most of Nova Scotia's good land was gone, and Prince Edward Island's land was locked up by wealthy absentee landlords. Cape Breton alone, of the eastern Maritime colonies, had good land available thanks to John Despard.

But Cape Breton needed more than land and smoothly operating mines. She needed roads, bridges, mills, doctors, and teachers. Who would live in a colony without these essentials? To get them, money was needed. Yet, in a colony without a house of assembly, taxes could not be collected. The British Parliament alone could do this, but British taxation of the Thirteen Colonies had led to the American Revolution. Britain did not want another American Revolution, this time operating in Sydney.

Despard solved the problem. He noticed the vast quantities of rum Cape Bretoners were drinking even in 1800; he reckoned around 10,000 gallons per year. If a tax of two or three shillings per gallon could be charged, the resulting income could build roads all over the island.[13] He had to convince the colonial authorities that such a tax was legal. He explained the necessity of roads and that if Cape Bretoners did not supply money for roads, the British taxpayer would have to do so. This argument carried the day and constitutional niceties were brushed aside. The tax was to be collected in the form of a duty "as a Measure calculated to preserve the Health and Morals of the inhabitants of Cape Breton...."[14] While it is not recorded if Cape Bretoners' morals improved with the tax, we shall see that their island improved as a place to live. As the tax money flowed in, the mines produced more coal, and land became available, Cape Breton was ripe for new settlement.

On an afternoon in early August in 1802, it happened. A 245-ton ship, *The Northern Friends*, sailed into Sydney Harbour with 415 Scots aboard who had heard, probably from their relatives squatting around Judique, that good land was available from a gentle, honest administrator in Cape Breton. All were intent on settling on the island. Despard was overjoyed; he quickly rounded up councillors, none of whom were in town that day, so unexpected was the event. Council agreed to use the money available from the liquor tax to "prevent their farther Emigration to a A Foreign Country."[15] Hence 40 shillings were lent, in reality probably given, to each man, 30 shillings to each woman, 20 shillings to every child over twelve, and 15 shillings to each child under 12.[16] The new settlers were given land near Mira and Sydney and by September were already clearing land.

Despard's fast action helped to prevent the Scots from leaving. This is a key point in Cape Breton history as the entire racial character of the Island would have been different without the Hebrideans. The latter were happy with their treatment, and sent back word to Skye, Harris, Uist, Benbecula, or Lewis that Cape Breton would welcome more Scots and assist them to settle in a home much like their own.

After 1802 therefore, more and more Scots began arriving. Despard gave money for new grist mills, so that food production rose dramatically; land petitions increased quickly as the Scots, who had never owned their own good land before, were willing to accept leases. By 1805, a new optimism was apparent in Sydney: a new market place was built for the peddling of local produce.[17] For the first time, Cape Breton could feed itself without relying on extensive imports of food. St. George's Church was finally completed: £300 was allocated for pews and a steeple.[18]

Meanwhile, Catholic Scots in 1805 began the erection of a wooden church where St. Patrick's now stands. A new surveyor-general was appointed to mark out urgently needed land boundaries; he was none other than Captain William

Cox. The colony's first surveyor, Captain Hurd, had been absent for fifteen years.[19]

So many people came that in 1803 A. C. Dodd, now chief justice, had to travel to Arichat by canoe to hear court cases of the growing numbers in the western part of the island. In 1806, the first meeting of the Executive Council was held in Arichat, with Job Bennett Clarke, A. C. Dodd, and Thomas Crawley present.[20] Land questions of course dominated proceedings. The island was now divided into eastern and western districts, as Scots began to enter the River Inhabitants, Judique, Port Hood area in growing numbers.

In five years the colony's population jumped from 2,500 to nearly 5,000. A whole new slate of people had come, and Cape Breton was now trilingual: French, English, and Gaelic, with the latter gaining rapidly on French as the majority language, particularly in the area from Margaree Forks to Port Hood.

The Scots fitted into the life of the island quickly. Shipbuilding spread beyond Sydney. Before the arrival of the Scots, Philip Ingoville had built ships near Wentworth Creek, in the area now called the Shipyard. While he continued to do this, shipbuilding began among the Scots in what is today Margaree Harbour, Mabou, and Port Hood. Between 1800 and 1805 the number of Cape Breton ships under sail increased from 217 to 267.[21] Most were small shallops or schooners which took coal from Sydney to Halifax or Newfoundland. With Cape Bretoners carrying their own coal, local money was kept home, thus benefiting local businessmen.

Despard sailed for England in 1807. The Sydney he left to his successor, Nicholas Nepean, was showing its first signs of hope, the first hurdles of settlement were past, pessimism melted away. His steady, hard-working, honest disposition shows him to be a man of great ability—one of the few administrators in Cape Breton's 36-year existence as a separate province of whom Cape Bretoners can be proud. His cracked tombstone lies unnoticed and unattended in Oswestry, England, but his term of office in Sydney will be remembered as a period when the foundations of the Cape Breton we know today were laid.

8

Anna Kearny:
An Irish Woman in Early Sydney

A TALK

OVER THE PAST NUMBER OF YEARS, historians—led by researchers such as Tony MacKenzie and Ken Donovan—have unearthed a good deal of information about the Irish in Cape Breton. Until relatively recently, the study of the Irish was neglected in favour of studies on the Scots, whose overwhelming numbers and influence had almost monopolized ethnic studies on the island.

The Irish are not the only ethnic group benefitting from the increased interest in the non-Scottish elements of Cape Breton culture; the studies of Elizabeth Beaton, my colleague at the Beaton Institute, in the ethnicity of Whitney Pier, and particularly her compilation of an ethnic inventory of Cape Breton, have opened new sources of information for ethnic studies.

Much of the information has been discovered as the result of clearly laid out research plans; other studies have come about by accident. The diary of Anna Kearny was discovered accidentally in a display case at the Public Archives of Nova

Scotia, and I waited over a year and a half to get a copy of the manuscript for study purposes. PANS know nothing about Anna Kearny; further research will hopefully reveal more than what I have been able to glean from internal evidence in the manuscript.

When the research is completed, perhaps one more piece of the jigsaw puzzle which is the Irish contribution to the culture of Cape Breton will fall into place. I say "jigsaw" because the Irish, unlike the Scots, never came to the island in overwhelming numbers; the potato famine which brought large numbers of Irish to the New World coincided with a similar famine in Cape Breton, so that migration was diverted to New Brunswick and the United States.

Accordingly, the Cape Breton Irish have come here in smaller groups or as individuals. The Irish in Louisbourg, the Irish merchants who settled on the island's southern shore after the fall of Louisbourg, the Newfoundland Irish who arrived in the early nineteenth century as miners in Sydney Mines and later at Lingan, or who settled at Ingonish and the Margaree Valley, or the northern Irish merchants who had a profound impact on the economic development of the island in the mid-nineteenth century, are examples of individual Irish who settled in Cape Breton and whose influence was far greater than their relatively small numbers would lead us to suspect. The task is to link the contributions of these groups together to get a clearer picture of the role of the Irish in this region.

Anna Kearny and her husband, Lieutenant-Colonel Francis Kearny, are examples of individuals from Ireland who spent time in Cape Breton and left a lasting mark. Francis Kearny sketched a view of Sydney from present-day Westmount around 1802, which is unique in being the only sketch we have after 1785 of Sydney as the capital of the Colony of Cape Breton, and only one of two views of the town before

1850. As such, Kearny's view is a perfect companion for Anna's diary, also composed in 1802.

What we have of Anna's diary dates from 1 January to the end of April, 1802. She reveals herself to be a shrewd judge of character and of the social scene, but one who is highly critical of social rivals especially of those who do not fit into her rules of proper behaviour. Her comments, often humorous, on the difficulties of transportation and communications, clothing styles, food and drink, the lives and attitudes of society—often unconsciously made—give precious insights into colonial life not only in Sydney, but in the entire Maritimes.

The Kearnys were stationed in Sydney with the 21st Nova Scotia Regiment between approximately 1799 and August 1802. As a lieutenant-colonel, Kearny was definitely in the upper echelon of the colony's society, and his wife and their children, Anna, Grace and James, mingled mainly with the elite of Sydney. The colonial capital, with less than 250 people, largely Loyalist and English, is however described in Anna's diary as an open society in which the people mixed at frequent balls and assemblies.

The entry for 1 January 1802 describes an open social gathering in Sydney:

"Mrs Despard [wife of the governor] gave a Ball in honor of the day.... Capt Cox was sent to inform us the Company only awaited for us to commence dancing.... I returned to the Company which consisted of all the inhabitants of Sydney both civil & military...there were a long set of Dancers...Ices, Cakes, hegus & a variety of refreshments handed about Cold meat for the Gentlemen in an adjoining Room & Trays with cold Beef Pye etc etc handed about to the Ladies in the Ball Room...."

More common however, were smaller gatherings of Anna and her husband with their social equals: the governor and his family, the professional class, the colony's administrators, and the members of the military elite. The following describes such an event, but the style of writing should be noted. Anna Kearny probably came from the comfortable middle class who were educated privately at home. Her style of writing and most of her social observations reflect her class's values and may be called British rather than specifically Irish.

"Monday 18 [January 1802]—M[orning]—Made a White Taffety Petticoat—E[vening] Having only myself to dress we were this night the first at the Generals, & had time to admire Mrs. Despards elegant taste display'd in the ornaments of the Apartment before the rest of the Company assembled—a beautiful Festoon of the wild Green moss of this Country, intermix'd with artificial Flowers, adorn'd the Pillars at the entrance, & had a most lively & elegant effect. rond the Room over every branch of lights were bunches of Evergreen interspers'd with Red and white Roses—the whole the ingenious work of Mrs. Despard, whose intention was to have hung festoons round the whole Room if indisposition had not Disabled her. ...most of her Guests exhibited new dresses & there were no absentees so that the Dancing Set was a very formidable one to me, who had not ventur'd out since my last illness—went down the first Rotation with General Despard & came off with flying colors—Capt. Weekes engag'd me for a second, but my back ach'd so excessively during the first dance as to oblige me to excuse myself from attempting the second, & to keep my Seat for the remainder of the Evening—Ices & a variety of other refreshments handed about between the dances, which were succeeded by elegant suppers in the Parlour & drawing Room—After which the Ladies broke up & return'd Home about two O'Clock, but most of the Gentlemen K [her husband] among the rest sat over the Bottle with the General till past 4 O'Clock."

Anyone familiar with the letters of Jane Austen, whose life roughly coincided with this period of Cape Breton's history, will recognize the style of the time, in the demand for elegance, in the separation of men and women for part of the evening.

However, the diary goes beyond the general style of the time and does reveal specifically Irish references and atmosphere. On 13 March she writes:

"had quite an interesting conversation with the General who I found acquainted with many of my old Irish Friends the Batemans Stoughtons etc etc — The Knight of [Glyon] (with whom in days of yore I have had many a pleasant dance) is I find marry'd to a Woman of large Fortune & so fine a Lady that he could not prevail on her to visit his Estate in Ireland more than once since their marriage — Lady Lumnsome 10 years back the fair Calisto at the Play acted by the Kerry Gentry in Kenmores Hall at Killarney now a Dowager at Bath who after 'a youth of Follies now spends an old Age of Cards.'"

BEFORE COMMENTING ON THE TEXT, its internal evidence indicates that Anna Kearny came from the southwestern part of Ireland and had upper class connections. The Lord Kenmore to whom she refers was Lord Viscount Kenmore, who had died at his seat in Killarney in 1795. Apart from this she reveals a sharp wit, this time turned against the fine lady, probably English, who would not deign to visit Ireland; her comment on Lady Lumnsome, the "fair Callisto," who now spends an "old Age of Cards," is equal to Jane Austen at her tartest.

I think however, that Anna's attitudes are, on the whole, more Irish than English. She condemns more fully than Jane Austen; she is more committed to propriety of behaviour and is less willing to laugh at it. Instead, she condemns. She is particularly critical of the wives of fellow officers. Listen to her comments on one family:

"Mrs Weekes & her spouse did not honor either of the

supper tables with their presence, as usual they toy'd and kiss'd to the admiration of Spectators, & return'd early to *finish* at home."

She had very clear attitudes of social behaviour. In another entry she comments:

"to the surprise of the Company, Capt. & Mrs Weeks chose to give *public* proofs of their contempt 'of *fix'd* & *settle'd rules*' by being partners in the Dance, as well as for Life & were as well in this, as in other parts of their conduct ridiculous to a degree."

These comments seem rather stern in a small colonial society where dancing partners were hard to come by and indicate a rigidity far stricter than one would expect. She reserves this critical attitude not only for the Weekses, but for others, like the Fitzsimmonses, miss and father, the latter of whom was arrested for writing disrespectful letters to the governor.

Lest we get the impression of Anna's being censorious and humourless, I must include one of many examples of her tongue-in-cheek descriptions of the hazards of life in a small colonial settlement:

"Thursday 4 [March]...Coll[ector of Customs] Moore & Mr Tate [a Loyalist settler] at Dinner they accompany'd us at Seven to Mrs Despards Card Party—a bad night & several of the Ladies ornamented with draggle Tails—Mrs Ritchie was oblig'd to take off & dry all her Clothes in Mrs. Despards Bed-Chamber before she was fit to make her appearance in the drawing Room Mrs Despard had sent her sleigh for her & the Seat being full of Water she was soon completely wet through Mr DuMerrich [Dumeresq] lost a pr. of shoes he had brought in his Pocket & drop'd in the dirt & Miss Green in stooping for her Patten's dirty'd her Silk Glove almost to the elbow in short many were the misadventures occasion'd by the bad Weather. Mrs. Despards remarks—there is sure to be a storm Rain or Thaw whenever she has Company...."

One cannot fail to get the impression that Anna was enjoying the spectacle of the colonial elite being discomfitted by the vagaries of the weather.

It is impossible to tell if these observations are peculiar to Anna or reflect the attitudes and humour of a girl from Ireland. What is certain is that Anna was conscious of her Irishness. Hence on St. Patrick's Day, despite illness on her part, she ensured that her daughters participated in the festivities. The governor, who had also lived in Ireland, called for a levee and Anna writes:

"Assisted the girls to dress & paid for it by an increase of Head ach went to bed very soon after they were gone. they return'd before one much pleas'd with the Night's amusement almost all the Ladies wore green Ribbons in honor of St. Patricks a few had *Shamourichs*—Anna & Dora (Cox) left the House with a bunch in each of their Bosoms but the former contriv'd to lose hers on the way—a variety of good things at the Generals but no formal supper—"

When it came time to educate her children, Anna sent them off, at a dollar a day, to a Mrs. Delaney's. We do not know anything about this lady, but it seems the fact that an Irish person was chosen to educate the children was not an accident, since there were at least two other teachers in Sydney at the time.

So the Irish influence was there, in military personnel, the governor's Irish proclivities (he was in Ireland when he learned of his appointment to Cape Breton), perhaps in social attitudes, and certainly in formal celebrations.

What is perhaps most indicative of Anna Kearny's ties to home was her longing for information from Ireland. She was constantly disappointed in not receiving letters, to the point of having nightmares of her brother's death. The anguish is palpable when we read:

"no English Epistles for us tho' December mail had arriv'd at Halifax from New York—wept bitterly at this cruel disappointment which from having had no intelligence of our Friends by the two preceding packets was totally unlook'd for & I foolishly made as sure in my own mind of Letters by the Express as if I had them in my hand—how to account for such repeated disappointments we absolutely know not."

Apart from an invitation from an uncle to visit during the brief peace of 1802, there are few other references to Ireland in the four months covered by the diary.

Research is still to be done on Anna and her husband. A possible reference has turned up in the *Gentleman's Magazine*, mentioning the death of "the wife of Lieut. col. Kearney [*sic*]" at Bath in 1818.

This paper has examined only how the diary reflects the Irish presence in early colonial Cape Breton. Beyond this, the diary reveals life in a colonial society and the strong character of Anna Kearny and adds a bit more to the emerging picture of the Irish contribution to the history of Cape Breton.

9

"Cape Breton's
Brief Time of Independence
Was Over"

1 8 2 0

I N 1807, John Despard left behind a colony which for the first time was showing signs of growth. Hundreds of Scots continued moving into the Mabou, Judique and Port Hood areas and were already filtering to the shores of Lake Bras d'Or. By 1813 the island's population stood at 5,975 as opposed to 2,513 in 1802; there were 110 mines (38 in 1802); and cattle numbered 5,550 (2,931), sheep 6,702 (2,677), and horses 413 (58).[1] Arichat was the island's largest centre with 455 people, while Little Arichat had 326, D'Escousse 248, L'Ardoise 189, and St. Peters 77. In this area most of the people were fishermen living on small plots of land of four to seven acres. On the other hand, areas around Judique and Port Hood, where the Gaelic-speaking Scots were settling, were composed of 200-acre farms. Already Judique counted 382 people, Mabou 232, the Gut of Canso area 291, River Inhabitants 270, Little Judique 185, and Port Hood 84. Most of these people were Scots; only fourteen adult males were natives of Cape Breton, the rest coming from Scotland. Already over 7,000 acres of land had been cleared on the island.

The growth on the western side of the island led to the establishment of a separate judicial region in 1808, with its capital at Arichat. With money from the rum duty bridges were built at Grand Mira and Arichat, and also at Wentworth

Creek, Muggah's Creek and at Sydney Forks. The New Brunswick Fencibles were stationed in Cape Breton after 1808 and were put to work repairing the Sydney-Mira-Louisbourg road; the old Baddeck-to-Margaree road was then begun, followed by the present Sydney-to-Lingan road. All of these roads were kept in repair and in 1815 a new road was opened between Stewart's Mill near Upper North Sydney and Bras d'Or.

In Sydney James Hill, the permanent schoolmaster, had his salary increased from 40 pounds to 50 pounds per year; a new dog pound was erected; and ferry service was inaugurated between Sydney and the Mines. In 1816, regular communication was established with the mainland when an Indian was hired to carry mail overland to Antigonish.[2]

Since Cape Breton was part of the Roman Catholic diocese of Quebec, Bishop Plessis visited here in January 1815. He had passed through in 1812, and even in that short time could see that in Arichat:

"There is a notable difference and considerable betterment. The houses are more attractively constructed and the people dress better. They eat better food...not that their fields produce more grain, for they [the Acadians] do not cultivate them, but because they have money enough to buy foreign flour.

"There is also much activity in the harbour. Many more ships carry coal from Sydney and other plaster from Antigonish. Some even go to the Strait of Belle Isle to gather from its rocks eggs of sea-gulls."[3]

Describing Sydney, Plessis noted that it then [1815] had a garrison of 200 men, who lived in a two-story wooden barracks which he considered the town's finest building. There was also a fort with twenty pieces of artillery. Sydney's population now stood at 300, a significant increase over the 95 of 1795.[4] Already some of the local elite like the Leonards, the Clarks, the Crawleys and Uniackes had found enough money to move to Hardwood Hill with its fine prospect of Sydney Harbour and healthy atmosphere, removed from the swampy land lying behind Great George Street. The lieutenant-governor had satisfactory quarters in Sydney for the first time when J. B. Clark's house on the Esplanade was purchased for that purpose in 1815. The house had seven rooms where the Council met and various officials kept their offices.

THE GROWING POPULATION of the colony seemed to ensure the quickening pace of development. Scottish immigration increased after the War of 1812 and the final defeat of Napoleon; in July 1817 alone two shiploads of Scots arrived from Barra with almost 400 people. They were given 5,000 acres of land near Grand Narrows and free transportation to their locations. These people were termed "the best fishermen in Scotland" and offered bright prospects for that industry.[5] By 1817, there were at least 7,000 people in the colony and two years later it was closer to 9,000. The population was growing so quickly that Hibbert Binney, who arrived at St. George's in Sydney in 1816, had a new Anglican Chapel built at Lime Kiln Point at Point Edward in 1818. The Roman Catholics established priests at Cheticamp in 1816, and another at Judique in 1818.

During this period the three staple products of the island—fish, gypsum and coal—were increasingly exploited. In 1806, 20,000 quintals [one quintal is approximately 100 pounds] of dry cod left Cape Breton, largely for the West Indies. Besides cod, pickled fish, fish oil, seal skins and lumber were exported. By 1814 fish was also being exported to Spain and other Atlantic colonies. Arichat in particular enjoyed prosperity due to the fish trade.

Besides fish, cattle and sheep and geese were being shipped to Newfoundland along with locally grown food products such as potatoes, reflecting the first agricultural surpluses of the newly-arriving Scots in the River Inhabitants and Gut of Canso areas. Even Sydney enjoyed some of the benefits of this trade. For example, in 1810 besides coal, she exported 2,600 bushels of potatoes, 78 head of sheep and 93 head of cattle, mainly to Newfoundland.

Gypsum also grew as an export during this period. In 1810, only 125 tons left the colony, but by 1817, Lieutenant-Governor Ainslie valued the gypsum trade at between 65,000 and 75,000 pounds. Ainslie allowed the digging of gypsum for a royalty of one shilling per ton. An acting customs collector had to be established at Port Hawkesbury in 1817 when 54 ships from Quebec, New York and Halifax alone took 3,696 tons of the product.

This period was one which was also favourable to the development of the coal trade. During the War of 1812 large numbers of troops were stationed in Halifax, so greater amounts of fuel were needed for their barracks. The problem was to get enough coal. Due to William Campbell's mismanagement the pits were full of water and the roofs of the pits were threatening to cave in. Moreover in 1810 the pit at the [Sydney] Mines was almost exhausted. The expense of opening a new pit and the rising cost of labour, due to the inflation resulting from the Napoleonic Wars and from the War of 1812-15, drove up prices of Cape Breton coal in Halifax to such an extent that the lieutenant-governor of Nova Scotia decided to open mines in his own province at Pictou. This frightened Cape Bretoners, who feared that Nova Scotia coal would be given preference over the island's product. However, the lessees who tried to open mines at Pictou soon discovered how difficult mining was and went bankrupt. This insured a safe market for the Cape Breton product.

Besides, as the lessees of the Cape Breton mines pointed out, "Coals are now found [1811] to be cheaper fuel both at Halifax and Newfoundland by nearly one half than Wood."[6]

This was because wood was becoming scarce along shorelines and transportation problems were increasing its price. Cape Breton's tidewater coal supplies assured a lower price than wood.

Since the mines could not produce coal fast enough for outside demands, Ainslie was forced to allow individuals to dig coal in places other than Sydney Harbour. These measures probably doubled the colony's coal output which by 1820 reached a record 9,980 chaldrons (a chaldron is roughly equal to 35 bushels).

THE POLITICAL DEVELOPMENT of the colony reflected trends begun during Despard's term of office. The call for a house of assembly increased and became the predominant factor in the political life of the colony. All four administrators who served during this period—Brigardier-General Nicholas Nepean (1807-12), Brigadier-General Hugh Swayne (1813-15), Colonel Jonas Fitzherbert (1816) and Major-General George Robert Ainslie (1817-20)—had to deal with the growing demand for such a body. Each dealt with it in a way reflecting his personality.

Nicholas Nepean was a weak vacillatory character, who received his appointment because of his brother's power in the Colonial Office. The parties for and against the calling of a house of assembly thus found him easy game. First Nepean fell under the influence of the pro-assembly faction led by William Campbell and Richard Gibbons Jr. He fired all of their enemies from office, but when he was warned by the Colonial Office that such wholesale dismissals would lead to his own recall, he dismissed Campbell from office and reappointed a member of the anti-assembly group to office. This pleased the Colonial Office and he remained here.

It was not long, however, before the weak-willed Nepean fell more and more under the determined mind of Richard

Gibbons. By 1811 he had convinced Nepean of the necessity of a house of assembly. Since the colony's house of assembly had not been called, Despard's tax on rum was illegal and Nepean suspended it. Gibbons then convinced Nepean to write to the Colonial Office asking that the assembly be called. Unfortunately for Nepean, the Colonial Office was more worried about the War of 1812, and had no time for a small colony's prayer for a house of assembly. Nepean was therefore dismissed and replaced by Brigadier-General Hugh Swayne.

Swayne was a man totally unlike Nepean. He was hard-headed, practical and stubborn. He saw his appointment as a mandate to improve the colony's defenses in the event of an American attack. Gibbons' pleas for a house of assembly Swayne saw as seditious in time of war, and he thought of Gibbons as an enemy agent. Accordingly, he dismissed him as attorney-general and appointed a Haligonian, Richard John Uniacke Jr., in his place. Swayne then spent his time organizing the colony's militia.

Swayne left the colony at the end of the War of 1812-15, perhaps sad that the Yankees had not invaded so he could try out his newly organized militia. He left the young and inexperienced Colonel Jonas Fitzherbert as interim administrator.

Taking advantage of Fitzherbert's inexperience, the pro-assembly group headed by Gibbons and Ranna Cossit Jr. decided to force the tax issue. Cossit as collector of rum duties refused to collect the tax on the grounds that they were imposed without a house of assembly and were thus illegal. Fitzherbert was at first confused, but finally threatened to dismiss Cossit. Cossit backed down, and Fitzherbert ordered him to collect back taxes. By doing this, he fell into Cossit's trap, since when Cossit tried to collect the back taxes from the operators of the mines, Ritchie and Leaver, they refused to pay and took the case to court. This was just what Gibbons wanted, for Chief Justice A. C. Dodd had to agree to the principle of no taxation without representation. The tax was illegal and could not be collected, and thus the colony was without financial resources.

Gibbons, Cossit and their followers had finally forced the issue, hoping that if the colony were to have any income, and indeed any laws, the Colonial Office would have to agree to the calling of a house of assembly.

Lieutenant-Governor George Robert Ainslie arrived in the middle of these events. A man with a quick temper and little sympathy for colonial emotions—he had just served as governor of Dominica where he had provoked a slave uprising—he was recalled and ordered to go to Cape Breton. He saw this as a punishment and brought with him a prejudice against the colonials. Moreover, he had a liver condition, and despised snow since it aggravated an eye ailment he had contracted in Dominica. As a result his stay in Cape Breton was a misery for him.

The Cape Bretoners responded by banding together against him. He was made to feel like an outsider and lamented:

"I cannot avoid remarking that the people in general here are so linked together by other ties as well as roguery that it is very difficult to bring guilt to proof, especially if the accused is a guilty defaulter; an almost universal combination is then made to screen him...."[7]

Hence Ainslie had no sympathy for the Cape Bretoners' desire for a house of assembly and wrote England that the people were poor and ignorant and incapable of operating such a body. Such views obviously influenced Under-Secretary of State Henry Goulburn, who had to make a decision about Cape Breton.

He conferred with his master, Lord Bathurst, and they came to the conclusion that Cape Bretoners must have representation in a house of assembly, but since they were too poor to support it, they would receive that representation as part of

Nova Scotia. In other words, Cape Breton was to be re-annexed to Nova Scotia.

Ainslie was secretly informed of the annexation plans early in 1819, and rejoiced in the decision since it would put an end to "The silly project of a House of Assembly."[8] He left the colony in the spring of 1820 unwilling to await the official annexation and happy to get away from Cape Bretoners whom he termed "the refuse of the three Kingdoms."[9]

Meanwhile, the people of Sydney were alarmed and sent an immediate petition to the Colonial Office begging that annexation be cancelled. They pointed to the colony's increasing population and prosperity and predicted that "Cape Breton's interests which can never have anything in common with those of Nova Scotia, will be neglected...." They added that Cape Breton would be a "burdensome dependent on her elder sister."[10]

The Colonial Office was willing to unbend a little and suggested to the lieutenant-governor of Nova Scotia, Sir James Kempt, that a special superintendent of civic affairs be stationed in Sydney to better protect the island's interests. Kempt rejected the plan, saying he would not allow his power to be curtailed and that Cape Breton had to come under Halifax's control as a county of Nova Scotia, "no different than distant Annapolis."

Kempt therefore received orders for immediate annexation and issued the proclamation, 9 October 1820. Cape Breton's brief time of independence was over.

10

Separatism in Cape Breton

1 8 2 0 - 1 8 4 5

HEAR, you Cape Bretonians, descendants of the brave,
Enrol yourselves together and freedom you shall have.
Master all your energies, and set your country free,
Despised by Nova Scotia, no longer shall you be.[1]

SINCE THE BEGINNING of the eighteenth century, Cape Breton has experienced a somewhat different history from that of the adjoining mainland. Geographically, the Strait of Canso has, until recently, served to isolate the island and has formed a formidable barrier to communications beyond its waters. History and geography have therefore decreed that any political union between the island and the mainland will be unsteady at best.

The story of the early settlement of Cape Breton was played out with mainly local actors, and the establishment of Louisbourg and Ile Royale after 1713 sent island history off on a sharply different course from the rest of Nova Scotia. Though politically annexed to that colony in 1763, Cape Bretoners were not happy with the connection, particularly since they were given no direct representation in the house of assembly, while being expected to pay taxes and serve in the militia. The Nova Scotian presence on Cape Breton was indeed tenuous, with only one magistrate for the whole island.

This frail link was broken in 1784 when once again the island was granted separate status with a lieutenant-governor, executive council, and a house of assembly—which was never called. The increasing population and prosperity of the island after 1800 led to the development of a movement for the calling of the house of assembly. The British Colonial Office, however, with an eye toward simplifying colonial management and saving money, decided that the Cape Bretoners should get their assembly as part of Nova Scotia. Consequently, a proclamation was issued in Sydney 9 October 1820 annexing the island colony to Nova Scotia.

The reaction on the island varied. In eastern areas around Sydney and Louisbourg, which had been long-settled, vested interests and a sense of island identity led to a persistent separatist movement. Areas far from the former colonial capital at Sydney showed far less concern. In Isle Madame, fishing interests who felt threatened by mainland competition, and officeholders who had lost their jobs, flirted with the idea, but the newly arrived Gaelic-speaking Scots showed little interest, if indeed many of them even knew about it.

The government at Halifax became more involved in the island's affairs than it had been in 1763. Weekly postal communication was established between Sydney and Halifax, the legislature voted £1,000 for roads and bridges on the island, and the land granting system was streamlined. Still, the citizens of Sydney were not satisfied. Sir James Kempt, the lieutenant-governor of Nova Scotia, reported to the Colonial Office that "everything is going well in Cape Breton...in short the People tho' generally poor are happy with the exception of a few individuals residend [sic] about Sydney."[2]

The Sydney people's unhappiness was understandable. As soon as rumours of annexation reached the capital in 1819, property values dropped quickly and money became scarce in anticipation of its change in status to a provincial backwater.[3] After the union, the population fell, depriving the place of its "most enlightened residents."[4] The reason for this was that most of the thirty office-holders in Sydney were dismissed by the new government, with the exception of the surveyor-general, H. W. Crawley, whose knowledge of the island's geography and land granting system was invaluable to the government at Halifax. Many of the former office-holders left Sydney; others remained, even if impoverished, to help form what the last lieutenant-governor of the colony, George Ainslie, called "a family compact" of separatists.[5]

Among the former office-holders, perhaps the most persistent separatist was the island's high sheriff, Charles R. Ward, who had been clerk of peace, deputy provost marshal, and member of the Executive Council before annexation. In 1833 he became publisher of the *Cape Bretonian*, one of the island's first newspapers, and he used the paper to influence public opinion. Ward's chief collaborator was Richard Gibbons, the fiery, irascible former attorney-general whose fight for a house of assembly had resulted in annexation. Gibbons was supported by his brother-in-law A. C. Dodd, who had lost his position as chief justice in 1820, and his lawyer son, Edmund Murray Dodd. Richard Huntington, the Yarmouth-born owner of the *Cape Breton Advocate*, married into the Gibbons family and was an active proponent of separation in his newspaper. Other strong supporters were Thomas Bown, merchant and collector of customs at North Sydney, and his brother Edmund who in 1825 lost control of the coal mines to the General Mining Association. Even the Reverend Hibbert Binney, rector of St. George's Anglican Church, had his reasons for opposing union since it would "reduce the stipend hitherto raised for the missionary."[6] Before annexation, taxes were not collected on trade items in Cape Breton. After 1820, however, tax collecting prompted merchants such as the Archibald family of Sydney Mines, shippers, mining agents, and lawyers in the area, and William Gammell, the chief merchant of the Boularderie area, to sign separatist petitions.[7]

While it is easy to see why displaced officials would support a separatist movement, it is more difficult to understand why such priests as Reverend James D. Drummond, Henry McKeagney, both of Sydney, Neil MacLeod of St. Mary's Church, East Bay, or John Grant, the pastor at Grand Narrows, were involved. One clue may come from Lord Falkland, lieutenant-governor of Nova Scotia. Falkland felt that Cape Breton's largely Roman Catholic population was opposed to his form of government which favoured rule by a largely Anglican Halifax elite.[8] Not all Roman Catholic clergy of Cape Breton were motivated by fear of Protestant domination, since some clergymen in the western side of the island were pro-union. At any rate, the separatist cause appealed to all classes on the eastern side, for in 1823 a separatist meeting in Sydney attracted "labourers of the lowest class" as well as "the principal people in this place, and chiefly the merchants...."[9]

Popular support for separation in the western areas was another question. The inhabitants of the North Western District (Inverness County after 1835) were mainly Gaelic-speaking farmers and fishermen with few Sydney connections; one observer noted that visitors to that area "hastened back to nuts and wine club and rub in the Capital."[10] The people of the South Western District (Richmond County after 1836) had received only a few roads from the former government of Cape Breton. A separatist confessed that districts outside Sydney had received very little from the previous government while being victimized by arbitrary governors uncontrolled by a house of assembly.[11]

Sir James Kempt, who visited the South Western section of Cape Breton in August 1821, received a "strong address" favourable to annexation in Arichat, the island's largest population centre.[12] This pro-union sentiment was demonstrated in the first election to the Nova Scotia legislature after annexation in November 1820 when four candidates ran for the two

Cape Breton seats. The winners were Richard J. Uniacke Jr. and Lawrence Kavanagh, both annexationists. They gained the vast majority of their votes in the South Western District, while their separatist opponents, Edmund Murray Dodd and Richard Gibbons, both of Sydney, gained all but eighteen of their votes in their home area.[13]

The results of the election showed the separatists in the North Eastern district, later Cape Breton County, that they had to sell their cause to voters of the other two districts. In attempting to do this, they used constitutional and practical arguments. They claimed that annexation had been constitutionally illegal. Their case went back to the Proclamation of 1763 which stated that King George Third "with advice of our Privy Council, thought fit to annex the islands of St. John (Prince Edward Island) and Cape Breton or Ile Royal...to our government of Nova Scotia."[14] The separatists interpreted being part of the government simply as being under the jurisdiction of a governor or governor-general and retaining a local house of assembly. In proof, they pointed out that the government of Grenada included a number of islands each of which had its own lieutenant-governor and assembly.[15] In fact, all other areas mentioned in the Proclamation—Quebec, Florida, Grenada, the Antilles, Georgia and Prince Edward Island—received their own government. The Proclamation of 1763 did not link Prince Edward Island and Cape Breton to the province of Georgia.[16] Therefore, by annexing Cape Breton Island to the government of Nova Scotia, the King was not precluding the island's having its own separate governor and assembly. Hence, in 1769 Prince Edward Island and in 1784 Cape Breton, each received a lieutenant-governor and a house of assembly, to be called when the population of the latter warranted it.[17] The instructions to the governor of Nova Scotia added that "due care be taken that laws, statutes and ordinances passed in our Province of Nova Scotia, that the same do not extend to our islands of Prince Edward (formerly St. John's) and Cape Breton, under colour or pretext that our said islands are included in this our commission to you and are parts of our Government of Nova Scotia."[18] The instructions not only guaranteed the two islands' making their own laws, but made the distinction between a province and a government, inferring that both islands were still under the government of Nova Scotia, but with their own lawmaking bodies.

These points were significant since they rested upon the royal prerogative or the King's power to deal unilaterally with conquered territories. When a territory was newly conquered, the King had the power to tax and indeed to rule it using his own prerogative. However, once a house of assembly had been granted, the royal prerogative no longer applied, and only the local assembly or Parliament itself could pass laws for the colony. Moreover, once the King had granted a house of assembly to a colony, only an Act of Parliament could remove the body.

This constitutional point had been decided in 1765 when the King had failed in an attempt to abrogate the legislature which he had granted to the once-conquered island of Grenada. Like Cape Breton, Grenada's assembly had not been called. Lord Mansfield, in deciding the case, showed that the King, in granting an assembly to Grenada, had irrevocably given up his prerogative in regard to the island. Only an Act of Parliament could change the constitution of the island.[19] The case bore direct relevance to Cape Breton which had been conquered, but was given its own assembly, which was abrogated in 1820. The separatists claimed that the annexation of Cape Breton to the province of Nova Scotia, by removing the assembly of the island through the illegal use of the royal prerogative, was unconstitutional and hence null and void.[20]

The annexationists, on the other hand, claimed that the Proclamation of 1763, by uniting Cape Breton and Nova Scotia, had granted the island a constitution, and had abrogated the royal prerogative over the island. Hence, except by an Act of Parliament, no further change could be made in the status of Cape Breton. According to this view, the 1784 separation of Cape Breton from Nova Scotia by royal prerogative was unconstitutional. It followed that the "re-annexation" of Cape Breton to Nova Scotia was no annexation at all, but simply a return to the legal status of the island.[21]

The separatists were convinced that this argument was superficial, and lost no time in trying to disprove it. Richard Gibbons travelled to England with a petition in 1820 and in 1823 managed to interest Member of Parliament Joseph Hume in bringing up the point in the House of Commons.[22] When this failed to elicit official response, a decision was sought from the eminent constitutional lawyer Henry Brougham, member of the appeals division of the British Supreme Court and founder of the Judicial Committee of the Privy Council. Brougham noted that "The Crown having given a Constitution to Cape Breton after its cession, including a Legislative Assembly, I am of the opinion that it cannot now abrogate the Constitution by proclamation annexing Cape Breton to Nova Scotia in the face of an express provision in the former Proclamation excluding the authority of the Nova Scotia Government."[23] This opinion became the strongest ammunition in the separatists' arsenal and was never explicitly refuted by any British official.

Though these arguments formed a firm constitutional basis for the movement, more practical complaints were used to gain popular support. From 1820 to 1845, almost every local problem was blamed on the union. Even before annexation, the separatists claimed that Cape Breton's voice would not be heard in Nova Scotia, since Sydney was 300 miles from Halifax over "a boisterous sea."[24] They were correct in their forecast in so far as representation from Cape Breton in the house of assembly could not keep pace with the rapid population growth of the island. In 1820 Cape Breton was granted two representatives for approximately 10,000 people and both members came from the South Western District. The number was gradually increased so that by 1840 each county had two representatives, giving six members for 40,000 people.[25] Given that Nova Scotia's population was about 200,000, a proportional distribution of members would have given Cape Breton an additional three or four representatives. Under-representation was a common plank in the separatist platform, and annexationists claimed that the separatists were merely seeking more members in the assembly.[26]

Another complaint was that Cape Breton was not getting its fair share of the provincial revenue. As early as 1823, Bishop A. B. MacEachern of Prince Edward Island, while visiting Cape Breton, noted that "All money for Grants, duties, Officers of Government, goes to Halifax. Even the emoluments arising from the coal mines go to the capital."[27] Hard figures were rarely used, but in 1841 separatists claimed that Cape Breton customs houses were paying between £14,500 and £24,000 into the provincial coffers, while island roads were neglected and only £1,000 was being spent on education.[28] Annexationists countered that Cape Breton gained £3,000 by being part of Nova Scotia in 1841.[29] Such contentions were difficult to prove, but they provided good emotional appeal for both sides.

Other separatist arguments were summed up in an 1833 petition and carried the standard allegation that Cape Breton money was being used to liquidate the debts of Nova Scotia which had been depreciated by annexation, and that Cape Breton was being "subjected to the Laws of another Colony, without their consent or their even being consulted."[30]

Petitions against annexation have been found for the years 1819, 1820, 1824, 1833, 1836, 1842, and 1846, and indicate that the cause for independence gained momentum in the 1830s and 1840s.[31] There does not seem to have been a formal organization of the separatists during this period. Instead, it was hoped that by calling meetings and signing petitions, they might reverse the decision of the British government. One such public meeting was called in Sydney on 4 November 1833 at which a committee was appointed, composed of leading Sydney area citizens, to collect funds to employ a council to bring a petition signed by "several thousand" people before the British government.[32]

The money was raised and a delegation met the secretary of state for the colonies, George Gordon, Earl of Aberdeen, at the Colonial Office in March 1835.[33] Aberdeen informed them that the matter was far too important to be dealt with except in a formal manner, and that another petition should be addressed to the King-in-Council. So another meeting was held in Sydney the next year and yet another subscription list was opened with "a considerable amount" pledged. This time the depressed economic conditions of the times prevented enough moneys from being raised and the bureaucracy was given a respite.

The following year, 1837, was no better, since at a public meeting in Sydney it was concluded that the rebellion in Canada would be occupying the Colonial Office's attention. In 1838, however, a copy of the 1833 petition was sent to John George Lambston, Lord Durham, who was governor-general of British North America.[34] He had little sympathy for any moves to fragment the colonies and agreed with the former Duke of Kent (father of Queen Victoria) that Cape Breton and Prince Edward Island should be united with New Brunswick and Nova Scotia.[35]

While wrestling with the British bureaucracy, the separatist committee turned its attention to the provincial scene. After 1832, Sydney Township was allowed one representative in the house of assembly. Edmund Murray Dodd, a separatist, was subsequently elected and he served as member of the assembly until 1848. Separatist pressure was applied to other island members of the assembly, with the election of 1840 being a case in point. The separatist committee met with Dodd as chairman. Various speakers extolled the possibilities of a separate Cape Breton, decried the illegality of the annexation and opened another subscription to hire a counsel in England. It demanded that the representative for Cape Breton County, James Boyle Uniacke, support the separatist cause. A separatist, Edward C. Bown, a well-respected merchant from North Sydney, threatened to run against him unless he came out actively in favour of separation. Uniacke responded not only by agreeing to support separatism but also by donating £250 to the subscription list, "by which he has forever silenced any doubts of his warm interest in behalf of the disunion of Cape Breton from the Province of Nova Scotia."[36]

Another important result of the meeting was a resolution to involve Richmond County more closely in the separatist movement. A delegation was to be sent to Arichat to stir interest there.[37] Richmond County's dissatisfaction centred around the province's fishing policy. In 1823, the assembly of Nova Scotia had granted a bounty of one shilling six pence per quintal of cod exported by Nova Scotia owned ships. This immediately put the fishermen of Jersey and Guernsey, who virtually ran the fishery on the south coast of Cape Breton, at a disadvantage. They complained, but were told that Nova Scotia did not have enough funds to cover vessels "not belonging to the Province."[38] The fishermen on the south coast continued to fight for the fishing bounty and in 1840, after a particularly poor season, complained that foreigners paid bounties to their fishermen while taxing British-caught fish. A large part of the problem was low prices. The bounties were expected to counteract the low prices and encourage Cape Breton coasters to fish off the more distant banks, thus increasing their catch.[39]

In January 1841 the Sydney delegation arrived for a meeting in the packed Arichat courthouse. They stressed that Nova Scotia was dealing unfairly with Cape Breton, particularly in the fisheries and revenue sharing. A frank exchange of views took place, with the Sydney delegates assuring the rest that their cause was legal. They even went so far as to advocate Arichat as the next capital of Cape Breton. Whether the delegates from Richmond believed this, they did agree that Cape Breton was getting a poor deal. Some felt however that increased representation could remedy the problem, while others were separatists. A committee was appointed to solicit Richmond County's views on the possibility of separation, and the Sydney delegation went off for talks in D'Escousse and River Bourgeois before returning home.[40]

This visitation seems to have stirred up interest in the western side of the island, but the signals were mixed. A petition in favour of union was raised by the justices of the peace in Inverness County. It was signed by 195 men of Judique and Margaree. Influential in bringing support to the union side was a Roman Catholic priest, Alexander MacDonnell, who supported provincial roadbuilding in this hitherto-neglected region.[41] A few months later, in March 1841, a meeting in Richmond County branded separatists as "office seekers and intending smugglers."[42] This contrasted sharply with J. B. Uniacke's contention that in 1837 only six people in Inverness and one in Richmond had signed a petition drawn up begging the imperial government to pass a statute declaring annexation legal.[43]

Separation was not an issue in Inverness County nor in Richmond, where the candidates for the assembly did not support the separatists. Clearly, separation was not a major issue outside of eastern Cape Breton. The *Cape Breton Advocate* perhaps expressed the views of the candidates returning from

Richmond County when it lamented that people there feared a return to the "irresponsible, arbitrary" government before 1820, when a few people in Sydney controlled everything.[44] By 1843 enough money had been raised in eastern Cape Breton to hire an attorney to represent the separatists in London. Petitions arrived there regularly: one with 1,000 names in January and another in July signed by 2,000, both calling for separation, and another with 550 names supporting the union.[45]

The colonial secretary, Edward Stanley, Earl of Derby, while professing neutrality, opposed separation; he asked that the law officers "report what course it may be proper to adapt with a view to maintain [*sic*] the union." He refused to give any assistance to the separatists' attorney.[46] He feared the separatist cause, confessing:

"I have formerly looked well into the case & the result was to convince me that the Petitioners are right in point of law. It would, I think, be ill-policy to deviate from the straight path of precedent & rule inn order to promote the objects of such Suitors. If they should succeed the inconvenience would be extreme."[47]

Stanley anticipated more than inconvenience however. During 1843 and 1844, the Nova Scotia house of assembly was interested in assuming crown revenues in return for payment of the civil list [that is, government salaries]. One of the province's most valuable potential sources of revenue was the Cape Breton coal mines, which were being operated by the General Mining Association. The GMA's lease was held by the heirs of the Duke of York. The Chancellor of the Exchequer, Henry Goulbourn, was negotiating with the heirs for the colony's takeover of their valuable lease. The resultant revenue would allow Nova Scotia to assume the civil list. The assembly was accordingly clamouring for complete control of the mines and the revenue.[48] If Nova Scotia should lose Cape Breton it would be deprived of this income, while Britain would continue to be saddled with provincial expenses. The lieutenant-governor, Lord Falkland, reminded Lord Stanley that "the principle [the legislative assembly's taking over the civil list] is established," but feared that the assembly would balk if it could not count on the anticipated revenues from the Cape Breton mines.[49]

Lord Stanley was thus in a serious quandary. The separatists' case had to be decided by the Privy Council as soon as possible. He wanted the Nova Scotia assembly to appoint a counsel to meet the attorney's arguments.[50] Despite Lord Falkland's endeavours, the assembly refused to name an agent, although they appointed a five-man commission to investigate papers relating to the annexation.[51] Lord Stanley overlooked this obstinacy and appointed a law officer of the Crown to represent the province. Stanley did this on the grounds that annexation was carried out by the British Executive Council, "an erroneous & illegal act I fear," and not by the Province of Nova Scotia.[52] He also chose to ignore Lord Falkland who wrote that he would be just as happy to be rid of the island since five of the six Cape Breton assemblymen were reformers.

The case was finally taken before the Privy Council in April 1846. The question was whether Cape Breton had the legal right to a constitution in 1784. The Crown argued that the Proclamation of 1763, uniting Cape Breton to Nova Scotia, was final and that it was unconstitutional for the Crown to change Cape Breton's status in 1784 by making it a separate colony. If the annexation in 1763 was not final, the same should apply to the separation of Cape Breton from Nova Scotia. Separation, the Crown contended, was a "mere experiment"[53] that was abandoned in 1820 when the government decided that a house of assembly could not be called. In effect, Cape Breton's right to send representatives to Halifax had been suspended in 1784 and reinstated in 1820.

Henry Bliss, the petitioners' lawyer, reiterated the argu-

ment that once the Crown grants a constitution it cannot re-
voke it. He did not contest the legality of the 1763 constitution, but contended that while a constitution could not be re-
voked, the Crown could divide a colony and then grant the
new part a constitution. In other words, the constitution of
1784 further defined the status of Cape Breton. If the Crown
could not do this, both Prince Edward Island and New Brunswick, which like Cape Breton had been made part of Nova
Scotia in 1763 only to receive separate status in 1784, were illegally constituted provinces.[54]

This argument caused a flurry of discussion and revealed
just how tangled colonial affairs had been in the aftermath of
the American Revolution. Finally, the solicitor-general, Sir
Fitzroy Kelly, admitted that "it is true that St. John's [Prince
Edward Island] and New Brunswick in 1784 were separated
from Nova Scotia by the Crown," but that, he submitted,
"was invalid."[55] In an attempt to prevent the constitutional existence of two more colonies in British North America from
being called into question, the attorney-general, Sir Frederick
Thesiger, submitted that those colonies' existence was legal by
acquiescence and proved the legality of Cape Breton's 1784
constitution.[56]

At the end of discussions the matter was not settled, and
the Privy Council's decision—that Cape Breton was unentitled to a constitution and separate status in 1784—was given
without explanation. Henry Bliss wrote to the colonial secretary, Sir George Grey, complaining of the performance of the
Colonial Office and claiming that the legal question was still
not answered. He went so far as to say that:

"The decision of the Privy Council must either be
founded on some reasons independant [sic] of that Proclamation [of 1763] or must involve in illegality the whole of those
four Colonies that once composed the old Province of Nova
Scotia."[57]

Earl Grey, who was new in his position as colonial secretary, scribbled on Bliss's letter that "I know nothing of the merits of this case, & whether Cape Breton has really any [grounds] to complain of what would render a separation... [justifiable]."[58]

Cape Bretoners had exhausted all alternatives except rebellion, which was unthinkable for a small island, but the roots of separatism remained. The former ruling class of Sydney gave up the struggle, yet even after they passed from the scene grave doubts as to the legality of the annexation remained. Cape Bretoners continued to be under-represented in Halifax until after Confederation, and economically they continued to feel as neglected as their roads, all of which problems they laid at the foot of the mainland government. This partially accounts for the later separatist agitations in the 1880s and in the twentieth century. None however has been so persistent as that following the first twenty-five years of union.

11

The Separatist Movement

A CONVERSATION

THE WORD "SEPARATIST"—Bob, we hear it a lot lately in relation to Quebec. Is this what we mean when we use that word in relation to Cape Breton after 1820?)

In a way they are similar: it was an attempt by Cape Breton to break away politically from Nova Scotia, which is what Quebec separatists would like to do with regard to Canada, because separatists in Quebec believe they are being put down economically, socially, and politically. Well, Cape Bretoners felt much the same way. After re-annexation in 1820, Cape Bretoners felt they did not have a fair number of representatives; there wasn't enough money being paid on roads and bridges; that the distance to Halifax was too great; that Halifax wasn't really interested in the problems down here. And then there was the whole legal aspect, which separatists of Quebec don't have on their side. See, the annexation of Cape Breton was not legal according to British law. The king had no right to just take the island and annex it to Nova Scotia.

(One thing the Quebec separatists say is that they are losing their language and their culture. Was there any sense that this was a Cape Breton concern in 1820?) What the Cape Breton separatists say is that our interests are different from those of Nova Scotia—but I think those interests are mainly economic and political. See, when you think of Cape Breton in 1820, the Scottish migration is just getting into its stride, the flood is

119

pouring in—and those people, most of them, are Gaelic speaking, and they don't know what's going on in Sydney. Sydney was the capital of Cape Breton between 1785 and 1820. And the greater part of the people living around the capital were either Loyalists or people from England. You have largely a developing population of Scotch, newly arrived and unaware of the problems—and a lot of these people are arriving after annexation. So the greatest centre of separatism you get is in the Sydney area where, after annexation, the property values fell—because the government jobs were lost. In effect, they were transferred to Halifax.

When Nova Scotia took over Cape Breton, they dismissed everybody from office except one man, Crawley, who was the surveyor-general of the island, and they needed him because he knew the island and he knew the Indians. Knowing the island was especially important, because the land grant system was in such chaos—and it was the fault of the Colonial Office in Britain. They had allowed land grants from 1785 to 1788 and then cancelled them. Then from 1788 to 1817 no land grants were permitted—you were only given leases or licenses of occupation. Then in 1818 Lieutenant-Governor Ainslie of Cape Breton wrote to the Colonial Office and said, Look, if you don't start giving out land grants, I'm going to start giving them myself. They wrote back and said, Oh, we forgot to inform you—you've been allowed to grant land the last two or three years, all the other colonies have been allowed to do it.

(So, when we talk about being separate, it does not mean Cape Breton wanted to be entirely autonomous from Britain.) Right, we were a colony. Moreover, we had a house of assembly. But it was never called. That sounds strange. When the colony was set up in 1784 by the Colonial Office, we were given a lieutenant-governor—that would be roughly equivalent to a prime minister now, who had a great deal more power

than he does today—and an executive council which was roughly a cabinet—a group of men who were appointed to advise the lieutenant-governor—usually wealthy men at the top of the colony, chief businessmen, doctors, lawyers. Then below that—we say below in our system—you have the house of assembly, where people would be elected to represent areas, as we have now in MLAs.

We were given a house of assembly, on paper. It was never called. The representatives were never elected. I know it sounds strange, but legally it's very important that the colony was granted a house of assembly, despite it was never called. (*And whose choice was it to never call the elections and never bring the house of assembly together?*) The Colonial Office. A number of people, including some lieutenant-governors, asked for the house of assembly—but it was considered the population was too small and too poor to support one. That was the excuse. They didn't think the colony could support a house of assembly in passing laws to make roads and bridges and so on—there wasn't the money to do it.

(*If the house of assembly had been called, what kind of decisions would it make? What would it do in a kind of benign way that would be good for the people of Cape Breton Island?*) As to the benign influences—a local assembly would be more cognizant of the local problems—what roads and bridges were needed, what economic relief was needed, assistance to farmers, changes in land grant system. And they would be there to handle problems more immediately. Their representatives would go to Sydney, to the house of assembly, if it were called.

(*Well, what were the threats and reasons that clearly Halifax did not want Cape Breton to have this house of assembly?*) Well, Halifax officials didn't want Cape Breton to be a separate colony at all. I have looked for evidence—for example, you don't see anybody coming out in the house of assembly in Halifax saying Cape Breton should be annexed—they are very careful about this. Besides, the MLAs on the mainland were worried about their own local areas. You have to look at what the officials are saying, what the lieutenant-governors are saying—and the lieutenant-governors like Wentworth are definitely opposed to Cape Breton being separate. And they are writing to the Colonial Office. And other officials of the Halifax government, chief justices and like that, are opposed. When there were arguments in Cape Breton between the Executive Council and the governor, they would often go off to Halifax with their complaints. And Halifax would use this opportunity to write to the Colonial Office in England and say, Look, this place is falling apart, they should be annexed back to us, the mainland.

(*But what was the threat to mainland Nova Scotia of Cape Breton remaining a separate colony? What did they think they'd lose?*) It was more what they wanted from Cape Breton. And there's no doubt in my mind that it's the coal mines that they really wanted. It comes up again and again. Wentworth writes to Henry Dundas, the Colonial Officer, saying that timber is disappearing from the shores for fuel, and the only cheap and easy source is coal from the mines. The Nova Scotia government tries to open up mines at Pictou—and they can't, they're not economical, and it collapses. So you have the only important source of fuel on the whole east coast, and it's in this little colony separate from them. But the supply was never certain from Cape Breton, because there was very, very little invested in the mines. Britain was very tight about that. Britain didn't want Cape Breton coal to find its way to New England because if it did, this would cause industry to grow in New England which would compete with Britain. Nor did they want industry to grow in Cape Breton, because that again would compete with the mother country. So Britain was worried about the whole situation of coal and the mining. And I think this is one reason why Britain did not want land grants to be given out, in case they were on coal. This is probably the principal reason she closed Cape Breton after the fall of Louisbourg [1758] and up until 1784—she just closed Cape Breton to all settlement, period—because she was worried about the mines. So coal in that case was a blessing, but it was a curse at this period.

(*Take me back a little bit. From 1763 to 1784 Cape Breton was part of Nova Scotia. Then in 1784 it was a separate colony, until 1820. How did it fare in the years it was on its own?*) The bit that's been written about that period—the Cape Breton colony has got bad press. It's largely because Richard Brown, who wrote the *History of Cape Breton* in 1869, was very hard on it. He was a "gentleman"—by that I mean he wasn't a professional historian. He was in charge of the General Mining Association here. And after he retired, he went back to England and he went to the Colonial Office records, and he wrote this history. He got bits and pieces, from what I can see in his history—and if you look at those sources and don't do a regular work on it, it would appear that the colony suffered a great deal more than it did. Because the colonial records are letters of lieutenant-governors complaining about the situation here. In my research, I've found that until about 1800 the colony has a very difficult time getting itself set up. Very, very difficult. First, you had an empty colony—very few people here. And then suddenly, it is said that a colony can be started here—and a few people begin to come: Governor DesBarres brings over 120 people from England; Abraham Cuyler brings in no more than 300 or 400 Loyalists. The supplies are minimal. Halifax gives one boat to help settle the colony so they can unload their supplies—but otherwise sends no food supplies, absolutely no help. And the locals allege that this is Halifax again trying to prevent the island from advancing. Jealousy. Ship captains are saying this. Governors are saying this. You could say this is a biased view. But I would suspect that at the very least, Halifax was not interested in what was going on here. And it is on the record that Halifax was not happy to see the whole province of Nova Scotia cut up in 1784—New Brunswick taken away, Prince Edward Island and Cape Breton.

Anyway, you've got these poor people settling here. It is a myth that Loyalists were all upper class. This isn't true. A lot of very simple people conscientiously could not rebel against their King. And DesBarres brought from England artisans, carpenters, stonemasons. So, very little money here. No house of assembly, so taxes can't be raised—this comes from the American Revolution; no taxation without representation—so they can't raise any taxes without a house of assembly. So all the colony gets is a small allotment every year—a few hundred pounds—from London. There are salaries being given to the civil servants and the military who are stationed here—but as far as public improvements are concerned, that's all there is. So you've got a class of people who are not wealthy, and a lot of them begin to move away—especially Loyalists. Not getting any government assistance, supplies run out. There's no money being put into the mines to develop them—so they don't flourish, and consequently business is not as good as was expected if the mines were producing.

(*And the governor of the colony keeps changing. How many do we have from 1784 to 1820?*) Thirteen. (*So, no decent administration here.*) No. No one to watch over the Executive Council who, as it turns out, are fighting among themselves. They, in effect, become the legislative assembly. They are not elected, but it is as if the Cabinet, today, became the debating centre, became like Parliament, and was split down the middle, as Parliament is. They'd fight among each other, and the governor would dismiss them for fighting, and he'd get a reprimand from the Colonial Office for dismissing them, would have to re-appoint them again—they'd fight again. He'd get dismissed, or move away. You see, you get no leadership from the top.

(*Do we get any accomplishments?*) Oh yes, things do start to get better. DesBarres is a forceful man who begins the settlement of the colony, and he does open the mines, against all opposition. Macarmick's period [1787 to 1795], the factionalism grows in the Executive Council and the colony is really in a state of decline, because Loyalists are moving out and you don't get any heavy influx of people. You get a few French from St. Pierre-Miquelon when the French Revolution breaks out, but not a big population difference. (*Does he keep the mines going?*) Yes, and he takes a lot of the profit for himself to make up for the low salary that he's making. And when Britain writes and tells him he's not supposed to do that—he quits and goes home.

Then you get a series of three governors—the last of these is Lieutenant-Governor Murray—who is a ruthless man. Comes in 1799 and is only here till 1800. But he's ruthless in a positive way for the colony. He won't put up with the factions in the Executive Council. Dismisses them, throws them out of the colony—but he begins building roads, like to Coxheath and around the harbour, does a lot in the coal mines, puts a better man in charge, asks that land grants be regularized—and, unfortunately, he was replaced within a year. This is typical. And I would say Murray more than anybody was the one who started to smash the factionalism. Now, Richard Brown's history makes Murray to be just a monster. Brown says the people finally petitioned to have him removed. But it wasn't the people—it was the enemies that he was firing. And Brown forgets that people like Ranna Cossit were in favour of his staying—they thought he was doing a fine job.

After 1800, things began to change, all for the positive. First five years of the century are very important. The world situation changes. The Napoleonic Wars are under way. The

French Revolution broke out in 1789, Napoleonic Wars by 1800—France is fighting with England. By 1805 they are fighting with Napoleon—until Waterloo in 1815. And this has important effects on this side of the Atlantic. The U.S. falls out with Britain over this battle with Napoleon—the U.S. wants to remain a neutral, Britain won't let her. The U.S. takes vengeance on Britain which, among other things, eventually breaks out into the War of 1812. It's interesting. The War of 1812 is almost always written as a battle of the interior—the invasion of Ontario by the Americans—but on this coast, we invaded the States, we burnt Washington—there were Maritimers in that group that burnt the capital. That's a facet neglected in Canadian schools. I attribute anti-American sentiment in central Canada largely to the invasion of 1812, whereas you get little anti-Americanism here, and it's usually imported from central Canada—because we tend to have a positive view toward New England, because of trade links and because we were the invaders in the War of 1812. It was our ship, the *Shannon*, which destroyed the American ship *Chesapeake* and towed her into Halifax Harbour. We were the victors in that, one of the greatest sea battles in Canadian history— which is not usually mentioned much in Canadian books.

Apart from all that, America fell out with Britain, and trade with the British West Indies was cut off to the Americans. That's when our ships pour down from the Maritimes and take over the market from the Americans. Exportations of fish from the Maritimes down to the West Indies to feed the slaves, pick up tropical products, especially bring sugar to England, pick up manufactured goods and bring them back to the Maritime colonies—plates and chairs—to major ports like Saint John and Halifax. Then they could be smuggled into the U.S. Because the U.S. was in a state of war with Great Britain.

The New Englanders didn't believe in the War of 1812. See, in the Midwest they were for the war—they were expansionists, and they wanted to move west and take over the Indian territories that Britain owned; whereas the New Englanders were opposed to the war because they knew they would lose trade—they were so much opposed that some of them wanted to secede from the U.S. This never came to pass. But what did come to pass was smuggling, and the officials of New England, along the coast, just looked the other way—manufactured goods being smuggled in from the Maritime Provinces. Or American ships would come up, load in Halifax Harbour, and take the smuggled goods back. Otherwise, New England would have really suffered. As it was, New England suffered very badly during the War of 1812. On the other hand, for us, this was the first positive influx of capital into the region—into the Maritime region.

Now, who's going to benefit from this influx? Well, because of the War of 1812, a large number of troops were stationed in Halifax and Saint John, the Maritime Provinces—and all these barracks had to be heated—and for that they needed our coal. So all during this period—from 1803-04 onward, as relations with the United States get worse, and more and more troops are stationed in the Maritime Provinces—the amount of coal needed increases. As Halifax and Saint John—and St. John's, Newfoundland, to a lesser extent—grow because of trade and commerce, they all need more and more of our coal. The demand for Cape Breton coal increases, to such an extent that they try to open mines in Pictou—but they fail. So there is pressure on the governors in Cape Breton and the people who are running the mines—sometimes it's private, sometimes it's government—to produce more coal. Finally, the government has to take over—it is a kind of precursor of DEVCO [Cape Breton Development Corporation]. It is interesting how privatization versus government working at the coal is a big thing way back then. So Murray dismisses the private individual and he takes over as government—he operates, builds a new stone wharf on the north side at Sydney Mines for shipping. He does a lot of this. The market for coal turns around. The War of 1812 brings in capital, and indirectly this comes to Sydney.

But the other thing, immigration began in 1802—the first Scots begin to come into the colony, so your population begins to grow. The Scots are hardly here and you check the shipping records and they are building ships and are fishing. There were no land grants but they were given land leases, and to these people from the Highlands, thrown off their lands—I doubt they made a distinction between a land lease and a land grant. Many of them just simply squatted. And I might add that the leases were never taken from them anyway; in the end they were all accepted as land grants. Another key thing happens—when Murray is dismissed, a new governor is appointed: Despard. He is the best administrator of the lot. Fate and personality come together. After a false start—internal fighting and all—he gets going and does a number of important things. 1802, he went over all previous land grants, and anybody who had left their land—for instance, there was a tract of land at the Mira River, 100,000 square acres—granted, but the people never came. He escheated that. That means the government just took it over because no improvements had been made. So this wasn't land forbidden to give out—it already had been granted legally.

He got this and a lot of other land, and he let it be known that land is available in Cape Breton. That's extremely important. And secondly, he did something illegal. He began collecting taxes on rum. Now there was no house of assembly—so legally you weren't supposed to collect any taxes. But he wrote to the Colonial Office—actually, I think that this decision had been made before he came to Cape Breton. He came over and he's here about a year and he writes to Britain: I think we have to have a tax here for the improvement of the colony.

I think the Executive Council and I should be empowered to pass this. The Colonial Office writes back telling him to go ahead, in so many words. So they'll tax liquor, for the morals of the people—that was the excuse they used to tax. The important thing here is that the letter from the Colonial Office, allowing him to collect the tax—never was signed. Signed by no one. Beautiful. I have seen the original letter. I know the clerk's hand who wrote it—but nobody signs it.

So Despard starts collecting taxes. Immediately, money starts coming in. He starts collecting in 1802, and in 1802 the first big boatload of Scots come in. They arrive and it's late August—too late for crops. Despard uses the tax money to buy them supplies. He gets them settled around Sydney and Bras d'Or. Well, word of this shoots back across the Atlantic—there's a nice governor in Cape Breton who'll give you supplies, good land is available, the place looks like Scotland—and on and on.

They come in 1802 because there's a lull in the war between England and France—the Peace of Amiens is signed—the war takes up again, and this keeps back a heavy influx. But ever after that, boatloads after boatloads are coming here. And by the 'teens an enormous inflow. They pour into Cape Breton. They don't go to Nova Scotia because all the good land has been taken up. They don't go to P.E.I. because that's owned by absentee landlords and they'd be no better off than in Scotland. And at this time, people are moving from Prince Edward Island to Cape Breton Island—because word is out. And they're getting leases. And with this huge influx of people, you see applications for grist mills, other local improvements. And money is available for these things, collected illegally, but regularly.

Despard stayed till 1807. But afterward, taxes continue to be collected on rum. And later, a cent a ton on gypsum. Rum was your main thing. So they'd make 500, 600, 700, even 1200 pounds a year. They set up a market in Sydney, roads, a dog catcher, mail service begins to Antigonish. Governors build better homes, a better jail, pay a teacher better, the Anglican minister gets some extra money—so times are better.

But this causes a political problem. Because you are collecting taxes illegally. And this becomes the basis for the new politics in Cape Breton, after 1800, where you get a man by the name of Richard Gibbons Jr., who is a young lawyer whose father had been chief justice, calling for a house of assembly because the taxes are being collected illegally. You get the basis for a party here. You may call Gibbons' position, the party of the left. Then you get another group, a lot of it made up of members of the old Executive Council, who say, No, there shouldn't be a house of assembly—because we can't afford it, and we're doing all right without it. So you've got two parties—a left and a right. And if we hadn't been annexed to Nova Scotia, I would say this would have become the basis for political parties in Cape Breton. (*Whether we should be run by a small group, or should we have representative government.*) That's right.

In effect, Richard Gibbons is like Joseph Howe—in that he's battling for some form of representative democracy. Whereas the others don't think we're ready for it, or they're opposed to it, or have vested interests—or there was the belief that people who have property should run the colony—not these miners and fishermen, who were almost universally illiterate. I don't like to preach history, that these people who were opposed to a house of assembly necessarily were wrong. This was what was going on in Britain—Britain was being run by an intelligent class of people. And perhaps they were right, that these people weren't just ready for it yet. And this question is, in fact, the Cape Breton political history until 1820—a struggle between these two groups for control.

It finally comes to the crunch—leaving out a lot of details—when Richard Gibbons Jr. convinces Ranna Cossit Jr., deputy collector of customs, not to collect the duty on rum. And the governor says, If you don't start collecting that duty again, I'm going to dismiss you. So Cossit backs off and starts collecting again. But there is a period when the duty wasn't collected. And the governor says, I want that duty collected. And the people who owed the most were the people who were running the coal mines—because rum played an important role in running the coal mines. They try to collect that back duty—and the people running the mines say, No. Governor Ainslie says, In that case, you have to go to court. So the mine operators go to Gibbons to defend them. Gibbons takes it to court—the grounds being that the tax was illegal. Chief Justice A. C. Dodd says, Yes, the tax is illegal because there is no house of assembly.

So with that, the tax money was all cut off. And in effect, the colony is bankrupt. Gibbons hoped the crisis would force the Colonial Office to call the house of assembly. This is 1816. There is a big spate of letters to Britain saying, We're in trouble now, what are we going to do? How are we going to get money? And the Colonial Office has to make a decision. They come to the conclusion on very little knowledge as to what was happening in Cape Breton—Governor Ainslie hated the people here, had nothing good to say about them, called them the "refuse of the three Kingdoms"—England, Ireland, and Scotland—the Colonial Office decided that these people must have representation. But, instead of calling a house of assembly for Cape Breton, it decided to annex Cape Breton to Nova Scotia. Then they'll have representation, they'll be able to get taxes—and this is what is done. Cape Breton is annexed to Nova Scotia by proclamation.

But the thing is—it's not legal. It's a long involved case, but when Cape Breton was conquered by the British after the fall of Louisbourg, the island was like booty for the King. The King could do whatever he wanted with it. What he eventually did was to make it a colony, and give it a house of assembly. Once he had done that, he could do no more with it. It's a limited monarchy. In other words, he's given them a constitution. Once he's done that, the only one that can change that is Parliament, the elected representatives of the people in England. But this annexation in 1820 was done only by the Crown— never went to Parliament, and consequently, it's illegal.

And this annexation, to the people on the left, looking for their own house of assembly—this was a terrible slap in the face. They became the focus toward a reinstatement of our separate status. They were the separatists. And this fight went on way into the 1840s. And it was largely supported by the merchants here in Sydney and Louisbourg. They felt that (a) they were losing government income, salaries, and (b) if we had a separate colony, these businessmen would probably be making decisions. You also get people of principle like Richard Gibbons, who wouldn't have much to gain from it personally. There are rallies, and many petitions over the years are sent to Great Britain—and very large numbers of people favour separation in this end of the island. And their attempt is to try to convince people in Isle Madame and later in the Inverness area—they are always sending letters over to try to get them involved. But they are unsuccessful. Out in the countryside, the only people other than the merchants who will have any influence are the Roman Catholic priests—and these priests were taking orders from Antigonish. If there was separation, they would break away from Antigonish—so most priests were opposed to separation. The only place you get evidence of any reaction toward or against separation in Inverness County is down around Judique and Port Hood. The priests there, Alexander MacDonald and others, are anti-separatists, and they won't let their people sign a petition. So the separatists try to make inroads *sub rosa*; we have letters of merchants writing to merchants—S. G. Archibald from the Sydney-North Sydney area trying to get William McKeen on the Inverness County coast to use his economic clout.

(*But all very civilized.*) Oh, yes. No war. No rebellion. It's all rallies, meetings, elections. It's interesting that later, when we get the labour troubles, we do go into rebellion. But I don't think we go into rebellion here because I don't think the Cape Breton personality is set yet. The Scots haven't been here long enough. The Loyalists and the businessmen are still big here— the English. The French are controlled by the Jerseymen, and may not know what's going on. (*And these men, while they wanted to rebel against this issue, did not want to rebel against the system.*) Certainly not against the Crown. There is great faith in the British Constitution at the time—tremendous faith. (*Which, had it been followed, we would still be a separate colony.*) Actually, that's right. Because after all those petitions, they hire lawyers in England, they make trips over—and it is finally brought to the Privy Council in England. In the 1840s they realize they've got to face this problem in the Colonial Office, because the annexation is illegal. And they recognize that it is illegal. And the reason for this being so important is that, during the 1820s, for the first time large amounts of capital had come in, the General Mining Association was founded. It is not because we're now annexed to Nova Scotia—the capital would have come in anyway at that time. It was the first vast infusion of outside capital to Cape Breton since Louisbourg. And if we had been a colony it would have been tremendous, because the money brought in steam engines to pump out mines, clean out the water, take out the coal—engineers and technicians came—they began spending hundreds of thousands of pounds. And if we'd have been a separate colony, the royalty from the coal would have come to Sydney, to Cape Breton. And every cent of that royalty went instead to Halifax.

In fact, so much money came in that coal became a chief source of income for the whole Province of Nova Scotia. Some of it found its way back here in roads, I suppose, but Cape Breton was so far behind the rest of Nova Scotia after annexation, because for so many years we couldn't build our roads—and such a huge population had come in, much more than the rest of the province. It was a developing area. The money was needed here, and yet it was distributed across the province.

The point is that a huge amount of money is being made by the General Mining Association, and this is going to up-keep the government of Nova Scotia. In fact by the latter part of the nineteenth century, something like forty per cent of the provincial income came from royalties of the Cape Breton coal mines. That money could easily have supported the colony of Cape Breton. They would have had both enough people and enough money to have a house of assembly. The money that went to support the province of Nova Scotia in the latter part of the nineteenth century would have been kept here to build. But it wasn't. The royalties were bled off to Halifax and the profits went to Montreal or Britain or anywhere else but Cape Breton. Just look at our cities. And as radical as Cape Bretoners have been—they called for not letting those profits go; socialism grew up here very early—but when you're lost in a larger house of assembly, you are always outvoted.

In any case, if Cape Breton breaks away, Nova Scotia is going to lose all this money and it is going to hurt them economically. From 1819 to 1846 we have petitions for separation. Something has to be done; an answer has to be made. This separationist thing can't just hang on.

So it was brought before the Privy Council. And the Colonial Officer said that obviously we've made a mistake. He writes it in pencil on the back of a letter. I've seen it. He said the complainants are right. (*The separatists are right, that they should be a separate colony?*) Right. But on the other hand, it's not convenient because it will destroy the economy of Nova Scotia. They go to the Privy Council behind closed doors. And the answer comes out, No, we won't take back the annexation. We'll never know what they talked about because no minutes were kept of these meetings. All we know is that it comes out—the decision is passed from them—says, No, you are not allowed to separate, annexation will stand. And once the Privy Council has spoken, that's it. That's the highest court of appeal. That's it, unless you want to rebel.

Legally, I think it could have gone this way: Britain could have said, Look, it's illegal but prepare a bill in Parliament and have it passed the next day, annexing Cape Breton to Nova Scotia. Parliament could do it. But I think they were worried about a big fight, because Richard Gibbons had allies in the British House of Commons. And if it was brought before the House of Commons (a) that a British colony had for twenty years been taxed illegally, and then (b) had been annexed illegally to another colony—well, it would have hit the fan constitutionally. I think they were scared to bring this to the floor of the House of Commons. So they made a decision. Fiat. Let it be. And there it was. And the Separatist Movement was pretty well crushed, for that time. And we've been part of Nova Scotia ever since.

12

"Poverty,
wretchedness, and misery"
The Great Famine in Cape Breton

1 8 4 5 - 1 8 5 1

CAPE BRETON EXPERIENCED dramatic political, economic and demographic changes during the first half of the nineteenth century. In 1820, the island was annexed to Nova Scotia; in 1826, the General Mining Association assumed ownership of the coal mines; and between 1802 and 1845, approximately 30,000 Scots immigrated to the island. This was a pioneer period, during which immigrants first came in contact with a new political environment and carved out properties to begin a new life on the island. The second half of the century witnessed the consolidation of these developments, as Scottish immigration ended and the settlers adjusted to the demands of their new environment.

This evolution was hastened by the disastrous events which occurred between 1845 and 1851, when potato rot reduced the island to a state of near-starvation. Potato rot, or blight [*phytophthora infestans*], which flourishes in cool damp weather, is a fungus which attacks the leaves and tubers of potatoes. First, irregular dark green to purplish-black spots form on leaves. Infected areas quickly turn black, resembling frost injury. Secondary bacteria and fungi often invade tubers, producing a slimy, foul-smelling rot which spreads throughout storage areas, resulting in the total loss of stored potatoes. This situation continues as long as dampness prevails.[1] During these same years, though with less disastrous results, since it was not as widely cultivated, the island wheat crop was frequently infested with wheat fly. This is a small insect whose eggs burrow into the wheat stems and destroy the plant.[2] Neither the rot nor the fly was properly understood or properly treated during the period under discussion.

Potato rot struck other areas during the same period, including Ireland and Scotland, resulting in mass starvation and the emigration of thousands from those nations. Nova Scotia, with its damp climate, offered prime conditions for the spread of the disease. It is not certain when potato rot arrived in the province, though it may have reached parts of the mainland as early as 1843.[3] The blight reached its zenith when most of the province was affected during the last weeks of August and September 1845, after a spell of wet, hot weather with unusually warm nights.[4]

In Cape Breton, the disease spread from west to east. The stored tubers were destroyed at Lake Ainslie as early as the winter of 1844-45, leaving no seed for planting that spring.[5] By summer, Port Hood's crop had "suffered severely"; one third of the crop at the Gut of Canso had rotted; Margaree claimed a 75 per cent loss; and the Richmond County and Baddeck areas were affected. The Sydney region, however, reported only a small loss. It appears that, on the whole, the rot in 1845 was generally worse on mainland Nova Scotia. By 1846, however, it had taken a firm hold on the island.[6]

Cape Breton was particularly vulnerable to the disease and its effects. The island was still in a pioneer stage of development, which other parts of Nova Scotia had left behind in the 1820s. Hence, "the poor settlers, if in distress, are not surrounded by old and wealthy Townships, upon the good feeling and resources of which they can fall back; they are often isolated, and if their own slender resources fail, there is no succour at hand."[7] They were made even more vulnerable by their dependence on a single crop: as one group of settlers wrote, "it is a well known fact the potatoe [*sic*] is the only article on which a poor man and family have to live upon for years on new back land farms in the island of Cape Breton."[8]

The immigration of poor settlers into the island had continued long after it had ceased on the mainland. The first wave of Scottish immigration to Nova Scotia, heaviest between 1783 and 1803, was composed of people of varying occupations, who had left Scotland voluntarily and who had travelled unassisted. Cape Breton received a few of these. Between 1803 and 1815, as the Scottish clearances intensified, poor and more desperate crofters, labourers and small tenants arrived, many going to the best vacant lands in Cape Breton. However, in the years following Waterloo, the kelp industry, which had temporarily supported evicted Hebridean crofters, collapsed under European competition. As a result, over 19,000 of the poorest people left Scotland, mainly for Cape Breton; this emigration continued throughout the 1820s, peaking in 1828. Finally, during the 1830s and 1840s, thousands more joined family members already on the island.[9]

Since the last-mentioned were the poorest and last to arrive, they squatted on what was left for them—the least desirable land in the remotest areas.[10] Abraham Gesner estimated that most of the 1,500 people who had arrived in Cape Breton in 1842 were squatters on private property. Often these people, after improving the land, would be ejected, only to wander elsewhere: "With a pig, a cow, and a few cakes of maple sugar, some are ready to migrate at an hour's notice."[11] Officials could not hope to keep track of these thousands who arrived at remote ports and who quickly disappeared into the woods.[12]

The new settlers had learned little in Scotland of scientific agricultural methods. They simply cleared the trees, burnt the wood for fertilizer, and with a *cas-chrom*—a home-made hand plough—planted their potatoes or some wheat among the stumps.[13] Fortunately, the virgin land bore abundantly. This poverty and overwhelming dependence on the potato proved dangerous. An extraordinarily cold season in 1832 greatly diminished the potato and grain crop. The following year witnessed serious crop failures at Baddeck, Middle River and St. Ann's. Though the government sent supplies, thus averting a calamity, circumstances inviting disaster in Cape Breton remained.[14]

It arrived in 1845. By 1846, potato blight affected virtually the whole island. This meant that lack of seed for the next crop made 1847 and 1848 probably the most disastrous years in human terms. In 1848, the rot was still bad and heavy rains after early August hurt other crops, especially hay. 1849 was a drier year and the rot was not as prevalent, but the wheat fly struck. Substitute crops, however, were then being cultivated, somewhat lessening the dependence on potatoes and wheat. The following year was moister, resulting in more rot which also affected tubers stored after harvest. In 1851, the fly once again devastated the wheat crop, and even in 1852, both parasites remained, though increasing crop diversity lessened the threat. Generally, after 1851, improved agricultural methods and a diversity of planting eliminated the danger of famine, though the two pests continued to be a problem.[15]

Throughout the period 1845 to 1851, generally speaking, the most recently settled areas suffered the greatest, since they had fewer resources to fall back on. Due to the nature of the disease, some potato fields might be destroyed, while nearby holdings were spared. The Mira River area was badly affected, particularly in 1847-48. The areas of worst infestation extended from there westward to the newly-settled regions around Loch Lomond and Red Islands, especially in 1848. Isle Madame's worst year was 1847, when the fishery also failed.[16] The interior lands at the Strait of Canso suffered in 1845, 1847 and 1848. The territory extending from Little Narrows to Lake Ainslie was very hard hit, the latter area in particular suffering successive failures from 1845 to 1848. Nearby Broad Cove lost its crop in 1845 and 1847, Mabou lost half its crop in 1846, and the 1847 planting was a total failure. Baddeck was hit early, in 1845, but in 1848 the entire area from the village to St. Ann's, and northward to Middle River and Margaree, was badly affected. The latter two areas were also attacked in 1845 and 1847. The Sydney area suffered most in 1847 and 1848.

The threat of starvation hung over the island throughout this period. When the blight first struck in 1845, farmers in Margaree hoped their cattle could be fed the infected potatoes, only to discover that the animals died. Instead, livestock was exported; in 1845 alone, Margaree shipped 440 head of cattle and 500 sheep to Newfoundland.[17] In such a way, cash could be obtained for the purchase of food and seed. Newly-settled areas could not fall back on this expedient; in 1847 at South Lake Ainslie and Whycocomagh, for example, when the cattle and sheep had eaten all the grain, they had to be slaughtered, so that seed grain could be saved for the next season. These people had given up on the potato, and should their next grain crop fail, they faced starvation. The same applied to Arichat, but as a seaport, oats and barley could be imported there from Prince Edward Island.[18]

Like Arichat, Sydney could easily bring in food, but the great demand for supplies led to serious shortages there. In June 1847, for example, there was not a barrel of flour to be found in the town, and a girl died of starvation at nearby Mira.[19] The danger of starvation was serious for the needy and the Indians, as well as for the newer settlers. A poor man starved to death at Cow Bay [Port Morien] in the spring of 1849, and a short while later a coroner's inquest found that a Mi'kmaw had died "from the effects of cold and want of food."[20]

No records were kept of those who perished from debilitation or diseases which developed in bodies weakened by hunger, but between 1845 and 1851, many reports indicated that people were in a "state of starvation," and that the situation in places was "fearful."[21] Conditions in Broad Cove in 1847 were described as "deplorable."[22] Such statements were commonly made in the house of assembly. A Committee on Relief to the Poor Settlers reported in the spring of 1848 that "Poverty, wretchedness, and misery, have spread through the island of Cape Breton."[23] The island was also described as the "Ireland of Nova Scotia."[24] People from the back and new settlements filtered into the principal towns in groups of twenty or more, some walking forty to fifty miles, begging for a bit of flour or meal.[25] A Loch Lomond woman later recalled:

"A group of men and women started for L'Ardoise by foot over blazed roads, following the lake and river down as far as Grand River then taking a blazed trail over L'Ardoise Highlands, for some of us were over thirty miles from our homes. The poor women were barefooted [sic] and each woman took her knitting along with her and knitted away as they walked over and around the hills, by windfalls and swamps until they reached the shore, hungry and tired. Each man and woman was supplied with a half a barrel of Indian meal, then they cried for something to eat. Mr. Bremner rolled out a barrel of meal and they rolled it to a brook, opened it and poured the water from the brook into the barrel and made raw cakes and passed it around to each person. All ate heartily then each man and woman took their half-barrel on their backs and sang 'Ben Dorian' as they left for their homes over the blazed roads."[26]

Other food-seeking expeditions were less peaceful. At times, panic broke out and force had to be used to prevent supplies being seized.[27] All over the island, starving settlers were begging for food. As the Reverend Norman McLeod so graphically described it, "the general destitution has made it impossible for the most saving to shut their ears and eyes from the alarming claims and craving of those around them, running continually from door to door, with the ghastly features of death on their very faces."[28]

The province had never faced destitution of such scale and duration. Incredulity greeted the first alarming reports from Cape Breton; the *Novascotian* speculated that stories of the loss of the potato crop in Cape Breton had been circulated to drive up prices. As late as 1847, the newspaper felt that reports of the disease were exaggerated.[29] The Central Board of Agriculture calmly reported that "no real distress, it is believed, will be produced by [the potato rot] except, perhaps, among a part of the inhabitants of Cape Breton...."[30]

The situation was made all the more uncertain since no one understood the causes of the disease. Some felt it to be "atmospheric; others that it is insectile. Some able chemists suppose it to arise from an excess of moisture, or from excessive cultivation. The Indians are of the opinion that 'Kesoult,' or the Great Spirit, has got angry with the earth for the wickedness of its inhabitants."[31]

The latter notion was shared by some Cape Bretoners who saw continual crop failures as a "Heavenly Visitation." The belief was particularly strong among Presbyterians, who saw the rot as "a judgement from the hand of the all-wise Disposer."[32] The *Presbyterian Witness* sermonized:

"It is, we believe, now generally admitted that the failure in the potato crop is to be traced to the direct interference of the Almighty, and is to be regarded as a punishment inflicted upon man for his presumption in attempting to introduce disorder into the economy of Nature by giving undue prominence to the Potato, to the supplanting of other productions of the vegetable kingdom.... We say nothing as to the ease with which the Potato was cultivated and the indolent habits thereby induced. Therefore in punishment for this abuse of his gifts the Giver of all Good has sent this disease of the Potato."[33]

The Reverend Norman McLeod saw the blight as a holy retribution for his neighbours' "unthriftiness, and offensive indolence; who can well feed and flutter, dress and dandle, and carelessly chafe away with toddy and tobacco."[34]

This disparaging view of the Scots in Cape Breton was contradicted by numerous descriptions, but none more simply eloquent than the plea for assistance from a group at Mira who wrote: "Your petitioners in the Country which gave many of them birth [Scotland] were taught to prefer industry with Poverty rather than idleness with luxury at the cost of others." Only extreme want brought them to the "humiliating circumstances" of asking for assistance.[35] Petitioners were commonly willing to repay for help, as the sixty families at East Lake Ainslie, who were willing to go on bond to settle for any seed or provisions, or the settlers in the Loch Lomond-Red Islands region, who promised to perform their own labour, if money were forthcoming for a bridge, so that they could bring oats to a mill across the otherwise impassable Grand River.[36] At Mira too, they asked for aid in erecting an oat mill, rather than requesting handouts.[37]

The immediate dissemination of food was essential in such an emergency. Early in 1846, the house of assembly passed a resolution allowing the lieutenant-governor to allocate £3667, largely from road money, toward the purchase of food for all of Nova Scotia. It was decided that commissioners would be appointed in each county to take charge of the distribution of supplies. They would take repayment notes from those receiving aid, which notes would be repayable to county treasurers. Reimbursement was to be in cash or road work, the amount to be decided by justices of the sessions.[38] The amount designated proved inadequate for Cape Breton; in 1847, the House Committee appointed for Relief for Poor

Settlers declared that they could give aid only where need was "almost universal." £600 extra was thus voted for Cape Breton County, £350 for Inverness, and £300 for Richmond.[39] It was intended that this money would be repaid by road work, but it was still inadequate.

The magistrates of Cape Breton County met in special session during the early winter of 1847, and four hundred family heads came begging for supplies, draining all local resources. When seed potato was distributed the following spring, the need was so great that it was eaten, and that which was planted largely rotted.[40] Consequently, in 1848, one observer declared that "not one person in every five hundred has seed of any kind to put in the ground."[41] When the hay crop failed and grain and seed were gone, people slaughtered cows and working animals, averting immediate death, but decimating herds. The summers of both 1847 and 1848 were wet and stormy, encouraging the rot and ruining the hay crop. Rust even appeared on the wheat in 1848.[42]

Many people did not even receive seed. Some living in remote areas of Cape Breton were not aware that it was being distributed. Others heard about the government programme, but when they reached the distribution points, they were told that they had been forgotten and that there was neither seed nor supplies left.[43] The Relief Committee finally had to admit that "the expectations of the farmer have been blighted."[44]

Starvation would certainly have been rife had people not foraged berries, hunted wildlife, shared food, or fished. Fishing was particularly helpful, especially in coastal areas, but unfortunately, the places hardest hit were a distance inland.[45] Moreover, the important fishery on the south coast of the island failed during the peak of the famine, in 1847 and early 1848.[46]

The idea of road work for seed proved unsatisfactory. Those most in need lived in remote areas where there were no roads.[47] Where there were roads, it was also soon apparent that the wretched settlers were not performing the required work. By May 1848, no road labour had been performed in Cape Breton or Richmond counties, prompting the Committee for Relief for Poor Settlers to observe that "the liberality of the Legislature has not met with corresponding gratitude on the part of the people—who have been willing to receive the benefit, but have made little return...."[48] In Inverness County, road work was performed in the fall, after rains had prevented earlier labour. However, people resented such work and it was poorly done, while the official records were in such a state of confusion that work debits could not be properly computed. Politicians furthermore complained that they were under great pressure to give assistance to whoever asked and were loath to exact repayment.[49]

The Relief Committee soon realized that "the benevolent intentions of the Legislature have been frustrated...." Not only was the road work poorly done, but the burden of paying for relief was also removed from those who could afford it. Though it would have been impossible for the local population to pay, the Committee was appalled that poor rates had been assessed in Cape Breton County only in Sydney Township. To the Committee this meant that people did not intend to repay, indicating a clear "relaxation of moral principle," which could lead only to "idleness and want of self-reliance and self-respect which elevates a people and enables them to overcome the difficulties and misfortunes of life."[50]

The question arose, however: Should the poor settlers have to pay at all? The *Novascotian* wondered why the citizens of Richmond, Inverness and nearby counties should be penalized with poor roads to avoid starvation.[51] James McKeagney, MLA for Inverness County [1843-47], carried the argument further by wondering why Cape Bretoners should pay for assistance at all when the government had given £1,000 in emergency aid to both Barbados and Quebec without asking for re-payment.[52] This point was sharpened when the lieutenant-governor, Sir John Harvey, placed £100 at the disposal of the Indian Commissioners for aid to Indians suffering from famine, again with no obligation of repayment.[53] The government never collected payment and reluctantly committed itself to large-scale financial aid to the socially destitute, setting a precedent that would be difficult to break in the future.

Besides government, merchants were called upon to give assistance. Great quantities of food were thus distributed. The managers of Gammel and Christie, merchants in the Bras d'Or area, recalled that during the famine they sold between 2,000 and 3,000 barrels of flour, but by 1853, as crops improved, they disposed of only six hundred barrels.[54] Either cash or credit was always demanded. An observer wrote:

"Any person possessing the common feelings of humanity, and standing for an hour or two on one of the wharves at North Bar [North Sydney], would really feel sick to witness the number of men walking about these wharves—running after the merchant whenever he appears at the road, as if he [the merchant] must have, and must give them Food. They see Indian Meal and Flour discharging from the vessels, and selling at a very reasonable price; but if a single dollar would buy a barrel, many of them could not raise even that sum. There is food to be had, it is true; but the means to purchase it is wanting."[55]

This shortage of cash forced settlers, particularly those in remote areas, to rely on credit with the few merchants who could afford to carry their debt.[56] Such merchants as William Kidston in Baddeck, Peter Smyth at Port Hood, and William McKeen at Mabou imported large quantities of food for the starving settlers. McKeen, who was the chief merchant of Inverness County, had dealings from Cape North to Judique. The Reverend D. MacDonald in *Cape North and Vicinity* described the arrival of McKeen's ship during the famine:

"At last McKeen's vessel with provisions arrived at Mabou, and word got quickly around. People gathered from North, South, East and West with empty bags and no money. A few had horses to carry sacks; the rest would carry loads home on their backs. McKeen hesitated to open the hatches. He told the people he could not afford to give away the cargo without pay. His credit would be gone. One Gaelic man asked what McKeen had said. He was told, and then came the exclamation in Gaelic, 'Oh Lord, how can we go home empty and our families starving?' Mr. McKeen asked what the man had said, and when told, he called to his men, 'Off the hatches, boys; we are not going to let people starve.'"[57]

Though the settlers went deeply in debt to these merchants, they all but worshipped them. Peter Smyth was later lauded, since he "never at any time refused an applicant for goods on credit, no matter how poor he was, or how impossible the prospect of payment. The calls on him in the hard cold year of 1848 were many."[58] The most valuable commodity the settlers could exchange was their land. In 1849 alone, McKeen received, for nominal sums, 1,100 acres and continued accumulating settlers' properties until 1855. An example of this sort of transaction is seen in the case of a settler named John McKinnon who wrote an IOU to McKeen for goods valued at £11, on 27 August 1849. Less than two months later, MacKinnon sold his 200 acres of land to McKeen for £15.9s.[59]

Most of these merchants spoke only English and came from outside Cape Breton. Peter Smyth was an Irishman who had immigrated to Nova Scotia in 1817; William McKeen had been born in Truro, and had made his money in lumbering before coming to Cape Breton; William Kidston was from Halifax; William Gammel, the chief merchant in North Sydney, was from Lowland Scotland, as was his partner, John Christie; at Grand Narrows, William Murray was from Halifax. Smyth was elected MLA for Inverness in 1847, the same year that McKeen was appointed Inverness County's first member of the legislative council. These accomplishments not only indicated these men's popularity and influence, but also their control over food distribution and road work allocation. The famine reinforced their economic power over the Gaelic-speaking Scot, and helped to make them his role models.[60]

Those who lost their land, or who were destitute, were often forced to leave the island. Emigration had already begun around 1840, as the best land was settled and the young were lured away by the opportunities in Boston or the Canadas. One observer complained that "the sons of our farmers, as soon as they are capable of entertaining three ideas, become restless and wish to leave the farm and paternal roof, and rush into some city or town, there, as they fondly imagine, to become rich and happy."[61]

The rate of emigration increased dramatically during the famine. Official records were not kept, but Abraham Gesner estimated that 1,000 young people left Nova Scotia in 1847; another 8,000 emigrated in 1848. A large number of these were Cape Bretoners; in 1851 alone, five hundred passengers left Sydney for Quebec City.[62] Large numbers of emigrants vacated the hard-hit Broad Cove-Margaree area for the nearest vacant fertile land, in the Codroy Valley of Newfoundland. Cape Bretoners had begun moving there as early as 1841, but their numbers then were "almost negligible." However, several hundred people left as the famine's grip tightened; the numbers declined during the 1850s, as times improved.[63]

Far more dramatic was the famous emigration of nearly nine hundred people from the St. Ann's area of Cape Breton in the early 1850s, bound for Australia and New Zealand.[64] In 1820, the Reverend Norman McLeod had led a group of Scots to St. Ann's, where he organized a settlement which he ruled with an iron hand. His community flourished until the potato blight struck and struck again. His son Donald had previously left for Australia and wrote glowing accounts of that colony to his father.[65] As the destitution increased, McLeod's fellow settlers became restless to leave, perhaps for Upper Canada.[66] McLeod, as leader of his people, began to feel the pressure to emigrate from this now "desperate and dreary place" to be with his son in Australia, "a kind of comparative Paradise."[67] The final blow came in 1850 when his potato crop was destroyed, "as black on the whole as any field could be during the worst years of that disease."[68] McLeod must have seen this as a sign from the Almighty, especially as one traveller claimed, "I examined other potatoe [sic] fields...and I could see no sign of the appearance of the disease...."[69] The following year, McLeod led the largest single migration to leave Cape Breton.

The years of famine also marked the end of large-scale immigration to Cape Breton. As the best land disappeared in the early 1840s, immigration had begun to slow, although in 1841 alone, 1500 of "these paupers from the Highlands" arrived on the island; in the fall of 1843, another "large group" went to Inverness County.[70] However, the flow of immigrants from the Scottish ports, which had averaged 6,258 in the decade from 1833 to 1843, suddenly fell to 2,939 in 1844, 3,339 in 1845, and to a low of 2,679 in 1846.[71] There are indications that a combination of extensive emigration and reliance upon the potato as a source of food were finally leading to population stability there.[72] The result was that large-scale emigration had ceased by 1844.

However, in 1845 potato rot attacked the Scottish crop, and continued to do so until 1851, with disastrous results. Reliance upon the potato had "allowed the population to build up to the point at which the sheer weight of numbers finally broke the dam, releasing the flood-waters of renewed emigration."[73] The number of those departing rose to 5,320 in 1847, 19,474 by 1852, and continued to soar upwards.[74]

Yet Cape Breton failed to attract a substantial percentage of these people. The distress accompanying the potato rot, beginning in 1845 on the island, was a prime reason for this. When the extent of the destruction to the 1846 seed potatoes became known, Sir John Harvey, the lieutenant-governor, wrote to Earl Grey, the colonial secretary, outlining the failure of the potato and grain crops and pleading that "pauper emigration" from Scotland be discouraged, especially to Cape Breton, "where distress is greater than elsewhere"; Harvey also warned that if there were another bad harvest, the situation would be as "appalling as that which now prevails in Ireland."[75]

This warning had immediate effects. Grey quickly instructed the Colonial Law and Emigration Commissioners to have mass-produced copies of the despatch distributed to all emigrant agents at ports of emigration, and to customs officers where no emigrant agents were stationed. The despatch was also published in newspapers, while the Emigration Commissioners personally instructed their agents "to discourage any emigration of labouring people to Nova Scotia."[76] In 1848, five boatloads of Scots arrived, but significantly avoided Cape Breton, heading instead for Pictou, where conditions caused some to re-embark for Prince Edward Island and the United States.[77] A clear sign of Cape Breton's reputation as a place to be avoided can be seen in the fact that the contemporary Irish immigration stemming from the potato rot there totally avoided the island, though 1,200 Irish arrived in Halifax in 1847 alone.[78] Cape Breton was to remain the home of the Scottish, not the Irish, Celt.

Though the blight continued through the early 1850s, its effects were lessened after 1850, largely because Cape Breton's almost total dependence on potatoes and wheat came to an end. As previously noted, the crisis of the famine years stemmed partially from the fact that new settlers had been ig-

norant of agricultural methods and the potential of crop diversification in Cape Breton. The Central Board of Agriculture
had fostered the development of agricultural societies since the
1820s, the first beginning in Sydney, with others growing up
later in Mabou, Margaree, Baddeck and Middle River. These
associations attempted to disseminate new agricultural methods, but before the blight, "not more than one farmer in ten
has been induced to enrol himself"; instead, Abraham Gesner
complained, "they choose to tread the old beaten track of their
fathers, rather than avail themselves of modern discoveries."[79]
As a result, these societies had difficulties in becoming established: for example, groups formed in Mabou and Arichat in
1821, and in Judique and Port Hood in 1823, folded or became moribund until the 1840s when Mabou, Margaree,
Broad Cove and Middle River began new societies.[80] Once established, these groups worked to enhance local growing conditions and techniques.

In 1846, the Legislative Committee on Agriculture decided to encourage people to grow oats by granting up to £15
per person to help with the erection of oat mills.[81] This fitted
in nicely with the desires of some immigrants who had grown
oats in Scotland, and who were now seeking assistance in
building such mills to supplement potato crops.[82] The policy
was successful, so in 1847, £30 was given to each county to aid
in the erection of oat kilns and mills.[83]

Though the potato crop was a complete failure in 1848,
the Central Board of Agriculture reported that imported turnip seed had been distributed and that the crop was flourish-
ing at Canso and Sydney, where barley was "half a crop."
Other crops included carrots, mangel-wurtzel, Indian corn,
rye, buckwheat, beans and peas, which were slowly taking the
place of wheat and potatoes.[84] In 1849, rot was not as bad as
previously, so in 1850 farmers once again planted large quantities of potatoes.[85] Yet the crop was again attacked, and disas-

ter was averted only by the unusual abundance of the island's
oat harvest. Also on the positive side, the wheat fly's effects
were finally mitigated by the late sowing of early wheat.[86] Even
though the potato was blighted in some places in 1851 and
1852, harvests then were the best since 1844.[87] After 1852,
crop diversification, better methods of planting, the use of ma-
chinery and chemical manures, the gradual decline of the
blight, and the introduction of rutabaga or Swedish turnip as
cattle and sheep feed to supplement uncertain hay crops, put
agriculture on a more solid footing.[88]

By 1852, the *Cape Breton News* could finally report that
though there was poverty on the island due to past crop failures, "there is...no probability of any suffering from want of
food this winter even amongst the poorest of our farmers."[89]
The Presbytery of Cape Breton appointed 28 October as a day
of thanksgiving for the abundant harvest at Sydney, Sydney
Forks, Mira, Catalone and Port Morien.[90]

Though the famine had ended, it had deeply affected
Cape Breton Island. It increased the wealth and power of the
island's chief merchants, devastated the new settlers, impoverished established farmers, put a fifty-year halt to immigration
to the island, hastened emigration—and forced the diversification of agriculture, which ensured that such a famine would
never again occur on Cape Breton.

13

Governance
in Cape Breton

IN 1784, Cape Breton Island was a separate colony, with a government separate from that of Nova Scotia. It consisted of a lieutenant-governor, an executive council and house of assembly. In keeping with past practices, the British government ruled that the assembly would not be called until the population of the colony was large enough to support it. Without a house of assembly important decisions on the operation of the island were made by the lieutenant-governor and the executive council. Hence, laws regarding the fishery, roads, aid to settlers and the general allocation of resources for development were made on the island. One difficulty with this system was that since there was no sitting house of assembly, taxes could not be raised. Most colonial income came from duties on coal, gypsum and rum. Since the coal mines were still in a primitive state with exports severely limited by the British shipping laws, the colony was always short of funds and arguments between the lieutenant-governor and the council were frequent.

As the colony began to grow, however, and its population began to increase due to Scottish immigration after 1800, a group arose that demanded the calling of a house of assembly. The British government resisted this until the group forced their case through the local courts which declared that even rum duties could not be collected without first being agreed to by a house of assembly. The colony was thus in danger of going bankrupt and a call was made to Britain to allow the convening of a house of assembly. Rather than do this, the British government, in order to save on colonial expenditures, decided to annex the colony to Nova Scotia. Needless to say a strong separatist movement grew up, especially in Sydney, that lasted for twenty-five years.

The main point of the separatists was that the loss of autonomy to the distant government in Halifax would seriously interfere with the island's development. They claimed that the interests of the mainland capital in Halifax were different from those of the islanders and indeed were often conflicting. These predictions were not borne out at first. Money which had been scarce before annexation, for roads for example, began to flow into the island. However, as the years passed some of the predictions of the separatists came true and kept alive separatist grumblings for 180 years.

First there was the issue of coal revenues. Just at the time of annexation, British rules on the shipment of coal began to relax, allowing the expansion of markets. The newly formed General Mining Association was given control of the mines and imported the latest engines to drain mines and raise coal. The result was an increase of revenue for the provincial government, which quickly sought to increase royalties from the mines to raise that income. By the 1840s, if Nova Scotia was to attain self-government she needed those increased revenues to support the government. Either that or face Britain's refusal to allow self-government to take place. It is no coincidence that the prime mover for Responsible Government, Joseph Howe, also called out loudest for increased royalties from the coal mines.

To Cape Bretoners, coal mine revenue that could have been used to support a local house of assembly was going to support one on the mainland. By 1845, however, the Privy Council in London had decided that Cape Breton would remain a part of Nova Scotia. The answer to this is easy to see.

By that time Britain had resigned herself to the fact that she would lose her colonies as they matured and rather than fight the inevitable, she would grant them self government as long as it did not cost her anything. It would cost her nothing if the colonies were self-supporting; hence Nova Scotia's need for coal revenues. Without this income from the Cape Breton mines, she could not attain self government, and both Britain's and her goals could not be met. Hence Cape Breton's interests were subordinated to those of the Halifax government.

An interesting comparison may be made here with Prince Edward Island. That neighbouring colony had once, under the French regime, been part of the colony of Isle Royale. In fact, it had played a subordinate role to Cape Breton, where the capital Louisbourg had been located. Its role was to feed Cape Breton and supplement the main fishery there. After the fall of the French regime in 1759, large tracts of land were doled out on Prince Edward Island to British troop commanders who, though most of them never resided there, used their influence with British governments to protect their property rights, including any attempt of Nova Scotia to take over the island. Hence Prince Edward Island was granted a house of assembly and retained its independence from Halifax, despite that city's attempt to annex the island. Control of their income has never left there as it did in Cape Breton. Prince Edward Island entered confederation as a separate province, a position, though with a smaller population than Cape Breton, it holds to this day. A logical question to ask is "Would that island give up its provincial status?" With four federal representatives to Cape Breton's two, and with two senators residing on the island to our present none, with control over its local budget, and a separate seat at all federal-provincial functions, the answer is obvious.

The situation by the 1850's grew worse. It must be remembered that there was no municipal government in Nova

Scotia until after Confederation. Local control of finances was at a minimum, subject to the whims of the Halifax government. Matters were made especially bad in Cape Breton since the island was chronically under-represented in the house of assembly. With a rapidly growing population its proportion of representation was always below that of the rest of Nova Scotia, while over-represented counties like Shelburne and Kings successfully blocked any increase of Cape Breton seats. This state of affairs simply fanned the fires of separatism in Cape Breton which, after the Privy Council's decision, was a hopeless cause short of open rebellion.

To make matters worse, until later in the nineteenth century, many of Cape Breton's representatives in the house of assembly, particularly outside of Cape Breton County, were from off the island. They could not speak Gaelic, which was the language of the majority of the people, and gained their positions because they could speak English and had strong ties with the Catholic Church with its powerful control of both the Scottish and Irish Celts, most of whom were loyal Catholics who still identified with politics in Highland Scotland and Ireland where that Church represented freedom and opposition to outside control. Many of these MLAs did not even live in Cape Breton. Elections were often mayhem, with political handouts the rule in the form of road work to the victors, and the cut-off from such benefits to the losers. This tradition spawned a mentality that has persisted to this day.

The danger of absentee MLAs revealed itself in the 1840s when the island suffered a severe famine, due to the failure of the potato and wheat crops for several years. The virus that destroyed the potato crops came with settlers from Scotland, where it was rife. By 1846 the virus had spread all over the island; it was especially serious in the newly-settled areas in Inverness and Cape Breton Counties [Cape Breton County then included the present Victoria County]. However, the whole island was in the throes of starvation since the fishery failed at the same time. The disease did spread to the mainland, but those areas had been settled much earlier, so they had a diversity of other crops to fall back on and the emergency was nowhere so great.

The difficulty for Cape Breton was to get this point across to the Halifax legislature. First it was believed that the whole matter was exaggerated; then it was claimed that the reports were simply ploys to get more government funding. It took over a year and the report of deaths for the Cape Breton MLAs to become informed of the seriousness of the situation in areas with primitive communications, and to coax action out of the assembly. The point was made that since the province had recently given free assistance to settlers in Quebec who had suffered a disaster, surely aid should be available to their newly-annexed brothers. Assistance finally came in the form of bungled road work jobs, loans, and grist mills for the grinding of oats, a disease-free crop. The money so raised was to pay for imported food. The situation was finally corrected by the establishment of locally-controlled agricultural societies which educated the settlers in the planting of alternate crops and proper fertilizing techniques.

The slow reaction of the provincial government to the famine crisis could not help but underline Cape Bretoners' feelings of powerlessness and disconnection from the Halifax government. Confederation added yet another layer of government that the island had to deal with and increased the powerlessness of islanders to control their destiny. When municipal governments were finally established in Nova Scotia in the 1870s, their powers were relatively weak and did not allow the island any more control of its destiny. The result was that in the 1880s the municipal government in Cape Breton County called for separation from Nova Scotia, with the MP for the area, Newton McKay, leading the charge. For over a year there was talk of separation, but his death from a heart attack quieted the movement.

As well, growing prosperity from the coal mines and later the country's first complete steel plant meant jobs and a temporary abatement of unrest. The remote power of the provincial government was replaced by the even more distant power of the owners of the mines and steel plant in London, Montreal and Toronto. The only way any local control could take place was through labour unions. However, there was little sympathy for unions in either Halifax or Ottawa at the time. As Cape Breton became more industrialized, the gap in the way of life between most Cape Bretoners and the marine-based white collar society of Halifax widened. Cape Bretoners and mainlanders grew apart even more psychologically. The loss of control over the island's destiny simply increased as troops were sent from Halifax or Ottawa to suppress strikes against the companies dominating local life. To make matters worse, the local university founded on the island had been moved to the mainland; even the seat of the Roman Catholic Diocese, representing the religion to which most Cape Bretoners adhered, was off the island, though Cape Bretoners constituted the largest number of Catholics in the diocese.

The frustration of lack of control during the hard times of the 1920s stimulated separatist sentiment once again. Strikes, protests over profits from the mines being drained elsewhere, fueled the fires of resentment. However, the Depression, followed by the Second World War, which brought temporary prosperity to the area, focussed energies elsewhere.

It was only after that war and the subsequent decline of coal mining, succeeded by the threatened closure of the steel industry, that the situation in Cape Breton became truly serious. The federal government realized that the province, let alone the municipalities of Cape Breton, could not handle the economic disaster that was pending should these industries suddenly die. It was then that the Cape Breton Development Corporation (DEVCO) was conceived. Its purpose was to slowly close the mines and to find replacements for the lost industry. The province in effect gave up a great deal of its economic control over Cape Breton to this Crown corporation which in effect was given almost *carte blanche* over the economy of the island. The irony of this is that in 1820 the British government had suggested that a special agent be appointed to help operate affairs in the newly-annexed island, but the idea had been dismissed by the lieutenant-governor who probably feared the loss of authority. Now in effect it was reality, with even less provincial control over conditions in Cape Breton. DEVCO in many ways became Cape Breton's own governing body and acted that way. Even the province conveniently felt that its role in economic development ended at the Canso Causeway. While DEVCO accomplished many important things, control over it was out of the hands of local municipalities as well as Halifax. Decisions as to its projects were made off island and out of province. Yet it was at least located on the island, many Cape Bretoners worked for it, and felt a certain ownership of it. As the years passed locals rose to higher positions in DEVCO and local input gradually grew.

The upshot of this was the further alienation of Cape Breton from the Halifax government. Indeed, in the scramble for new jobs Halifax, which had been declared a growth centre by government, was seen as Cape Breton's rival in the quest for new industry. Halifax, on the other hand, felt that Cape Breton had been singled out for special favours.

In the midst of this growing tension Cape Breton entered a cultural renaissance with the flowering of its music and art; it gained a new university; books were being published on the island. The Cape Breton sense of separate identity sharpened. Enterprise Cape Breton Corporation (ECBC) succeeded DEVCO as the federal government's arm of economic development on the island and teamed up with the community and local university in a much closer way than DEVCO had done, giving at least the illusion of local control. ECBC's presence only heightened the island's sense of separate identity.

It is not surprising therefore that as economic conditions worsened, Cape Breton separatist tendencies arose in the 1970s, 1980s, and now, at the turn of the twenty-first century. Economic development seems to have failed and as a result people seek greater control of their destiny. Yet the only form of democratic government over which they have complete local control is at the municipal level, which is powerless, overburdened by increasing financial responsibilities devolving upon them by the Halifax government. The question was, and is, how can the municipalities of the island come together to better control the economy and destiny of Cape Breton? How can their power be increased so that they can have a greater say in their own destiny short of outright separation from Nova Scotia? As long as these questions remain unanswered Cape Breton will languish economically, separatist talk will not go away, federal and provincial politicians will try to outdo each other in blaming each other's level of government for the island's economic woes, and federally initiated economic development agencies will fail.

NOTES

1. J. F. W. DesBarres, the Founder 1784-1787

1 For a fuller discussion of the organization of the colony of Cape Breton, see R.J. Morgan, *Orphan Outpost: Cape Breton Colony 1784-1820* (Ph.D. thesis, University of Ottawa, 1972).

2 The Navigation Laws were passed to confine British commerce to that nation's vessels and colonial possessions. Certain strategic commodities, such as coal, could not be shipped to foreign countries. The purpose of the laws was the aggrandizement of Britain's economy.

3 DesBarres had a small book published justifying his policies in Cape Breton in answer to Dr. William Smith, an executive councillor who wrote a pamphlet attacking him. The book gives an excellent insight into DesBarres's character and is entitled *Letter to Lord...on a Caveat against Emigration to America.* In North America, copies are available at the Public Archives of Nova Scotia (hereafter PANS); the Public Archives of Canada (hereafter PAC); the Beaton Institute, University College of Cape Breton (hereafter Beaton Institute); and Harvard University.

4 Colonial Office Papers (hereafter C.O.) Series 216, B 1, 25 July 1785, pp. 3-12.

5 Sydney to DesBarres, 30 November 1786, C.O. 218, vol. 12, pp. 10-12.

6 Sydney to DesBarres, 20 February 1785, DesBarres papers, M.G. 23, I, vol. 4, pp. 772-772, PAC; Sydney to DesBarres, 25 March 1784, *ibid.*, pp. 782-785.

7 G.N.D. Evans, *Uncommon Obdurate: The Several Public Careers of J.F.W. DesBarres* (Salem, Mass. and Toronto, 1969) pp. 49-51.

8 The issue of the location of the whale fishery is discussed more completely in C.R. Fergusson, "The Southern Whale Fishery 1775-1804" *Collections* of the Nova Scotia Historical Society, XXXII (1959) 79, 124.

9 Michael H. Berne, "The Origin of Colonial Settlements in the Maritimes," Plan 1 (1960) 103.

10 Sydney to DesBarres, 30 November 1786, C.O. 218, vol. 12, f. 1012.

3. The Loyalists of Cape Breton

1 William Knox to William Falkener, 5 July 1804, C.O. 323/176, ff. 234-239.

2 D.C. Harvey, ed., *Holland's Description of Cape Breton Island and Other Documents*, PANS, 1935, p. 10.

3 *Ibid.*, p. 85.

4   Haldimand to Lord Sydney, 25 October 1782, M.G. 21, Q 20, pp. 310-316.

5   A Memorial of A. Cuyler to the Lords Commissioners of Treasury, 30 March 1781, Audit Office 13, Bundle 109.

6   Minutes of the Executive Council of Cape Breton (hereafter C.B. B) 4 July 1789. Investigation into the Conduct of Abraham Cuyler, C.B. B 5, pp. 249-258.

7   Investigation..., 31 July 1789, C.B. B 6, pp. 119-124; Audit Office 13/13, ff. 496-507; L. Sabine, *Biographical Sketches of Loyalists of the American Revolution* (Boston: Little Brown, 1864).

8   The best study of DesBarres's many accomplishments is G.N.D. Evans, *Uncommon Obdurate: The Several Public Careers of J.F.W. DesBarres* (Toronto: University Press, 1969).

9   DesBarres to Lord North, 16 May 1783, Windham Papers, Additional Manuscripts 37, 890, ff. 28-30.

10   Remarks by DesBarres on a copy of a letter from Evan Nepean (Undersecretary of State) to DesBarres, 2 July 1784, Windham Papers, *ibid.*, f. 36.

11   Sydney to Haldimand, 7 June 1784, British Museum, Additional Manuscripts 21, 710, pp. 175-176.

12   Parr to Cuyler, 13 September 1784, C.B. A 7, pp. 25-26.

13   E. Jackson, *Cape Breton and the Jackson Kith and Kin* (Windsor: Lancelot Press, 1971) p. 60. Other examples include Joseph Hart, Moses Huel and Ingram Ball who did not arrive in Cape Breton until 1808.

14   Campbell to Sydney, enclosure in a letter 30 November 1785, N.S. A 107, p. 375.

15   Deposition of Terrence McCorristine, 5 June 1786, C.B. A 3, pp. 101-102.

16   Richard Brown, *A History of the Island of Cape Breton* (London: Sampson Low, 1869) p. 392.

17   [Nepean] to Haldimand, 7 June 1784, M.G. 11, Q 23, pp. 91-94.

18   E. Jackson, *op. cit.*, J.F. Hart, *History of North East Margaree* (private printing, 1963).

19   Women's Institute of Mira Gut, *A Brief History of Mira Gut (1745-1968)* (private printing) p. 9.

20   Notes of Thomas Ashfield (DesBarres' Secretary), DesBarres Papers, M.G. 23, F 1, Series 4, p. 23.

21   L. Sabine, *op.cit.*, vol. 2, pp. 51-52.

22   R.J. Morgan, *Orphan Outpost: Cape Breton Colony 1784-1820* (Ph.D. thesis, University of Ottawa, 1972).

23   Lord Sydney accused DesBarres of this, and he was probably correct, moral considerations aside. Sydney to DesBarres, 30 November 1787, C.O. 218, vol. 12, ff. 10-12.

24   G.N.D. Evans, *op. cit.*, p. 55.

25   Extract of the Journal of Lieutenant Norford, 20 March 1786, C.B. A 12, pp. 156-165.

26   "Remonstrance and Petition of the Principle Inhabitants of the Island of Cape Breton," DesBarres Papers, *op. cit.*, vol. 2, pp. 370-371.

27 Richard Gibbons (1734-1794) had served as Attorney-General of Nova Scotia before coming to Sydney.

28 Lieutenant-Governor William Macarmick to Evan Nepean, 18 May 1790, C.B. A 17, p. 125.

29 Macarmick to Dundas, 19 May 1794, C.B. A 12, pp. 52-53.

30 Mathews to Macarmick, 13 August 1794, *ibid.*, p. 162.

31 Mathews to E. Nepean, 10 June 1786, C.B. A 3, pp. 105-110.

32 Macarmick retained his position of lieutenant-governor until his death in 1815 even though he left the island in 1795. In the interim the colony was run by administrators who had the same powers as a lieutenant-governor. The third lieutenant-governor, George Robert Ainslie, was appointed in 1815.

33 Saint George's Church Registry, Beaton Institute, Sydney, C.B., p. 15.

34 *Ibid.*, p. 8.

35 Council, 1 August 1798, C.O. 217, vol. 115, ff. 216-218.

36 Cossit to the Society for the Propagation of the Gospel (hereafter SPG), 9 March 1796, SPG Papers, vol. 27, pp. 64-68.

37 Inglis' diary of his visit to Cape Breton, 7 July 1805, Inglis Papers, M.G. 23, C 6, vol. 6.

38 Richard Gibbons, Junior, had been captured with his father by a French ship on a voyage to England in 1792. They were taken prisoners to France where Judge Gibbons died in 1794. In 1796, young Gibbons was back in Sydney.

39 Draft of a letter, A.C. Dodd to Swayne, 8 April 1813, Dodd Papers, doc. 84, PANS.

40 Fitzherbert to Lord Bathurst, 18 May 1816, C.O. 217, vol. 134, ff. 9-10.

41 R.J. Uniacke, Report of the Trial of Ritchie and Leaver, *ibid.*, f. 30.

42 *Ibid.*, f. 33.

43 Ainslie to Henry Goulbourn (private), 15 February 1820, *ibid.*, vol. 138, f. 30.

44 J.G. McKinnon, *Old Sydney* (Sydney: McKinnon, 1918) p. 130.

45 See above, fn. 18.

46 W.S. MacNutt, *The Atlantic Provinces: The Emergence of Colonial Society 1712-1857* (Toronto: McClelland and Stewart, 1965).

5. Ranna Cossit: The Loyalist Rector of St. George's Church

1 O.G. Hammond, *Tories of New Hampshire in the War of the Revolution* (Concord, 1917) p. 26.

2 Mason Wade, "Odyssey of a Loyalist Rector," *Vermont History*, XLVIII, 2 (Spring, 1980), p. 100.

3 Pearl S. Cossit, *The Cossit Family* (Pasadena, California), *Genealogical and Family History of the State of New Hampshire*, vol. 1 (New York, 1908).

4 Robert J. Morgan, *Orphan Outpost: Cape Breton Colony 1784-1820* (Ph.D. thesis, University of Ottawa, 1972).

5 "The Reverend Ranna Cossit," *The Journal of the Canadian Church Historical Society*, V, 3 (September 1963), n.p.

6 Franklynn MacLean, "The Reverend Ranna Cossit," in R. Morgan, ed. *More*

Essays in Cape Breton History (Windsor, N.S., 1977) pp. 66-67.

7 Ranna Cossit, *Letter Book*, June 1786, Cossit House, Sydney, C.B.; Archdeacon A. Smith, "The First Seventy Years of St. George's Parish," *The Cape Breton Historical Society* (Sydney, 1932).

8 PAC, Cape Breton A vol. 12, petition enclosed in Macarmick to Dundas, 18 July 1794.

9 St. George's Anglican Church, Sydney, C.B., Death Records.

7. Cape Breton's Debt to John Despard

1 George Moore to Earl Camden, 21 November 1804, C.O. 217, vol. 122, f. 132.

2 *Gentleman's Magazine* (October 1829), 369-370; *The Royal Military Calendar* (1816), I, 129-130; *Dictionary of National Biography*, V (1964), 859-860.

3 David Mathews held public office in New York. In 1782 he had been appointed Registrar of the Admiralty Court. He maintained two establishments which were both confiscated by the new Republic. L. Sabine, *Biographical Sketches of Loyalists of the American Revolution* (Boston, 1864) II, 51-52; Sir William Howe to Lord Sydney, 1784, C.O. 217, vol. 114, ff. 134-135.

4 Abraham Cuyler had been placed in charge of refugee Loyalists in Montreal in 1782, and it was there that he probably met Samuel Holland, who had surveyed Cape Breton 1765-1768, and who was sanguine about the settlement of Loyalists on the Island. Memorial of A. Cuyler to the Lords Commissioners of Treasury, 30 March 1781, A.O. 13, Bundle 109; General Haldimand to the Lords Commissioners of the Treasury, 30 March 1781, A.O. 13/109.

5 Ingram Ball was a Loyalist who had served in the 7th Dragoons in America and settled around 1788 at Ball's Creek near Sydney. Ball to Evan Nepean, 26 July 1792, Cape Breton A 10, p. 86; Ball to the Duke of Portland, 10 September 1795, C.O. 217, vol. 3, ff. 200-201; Ogilvie to Portland, 10 January 1799, *ibid.*, vol. 117, f. 21.

6 William McKinnon was a southern Loyalist who had served in the Carolina Regiment during the American Revolution and had lost £7,900. McKinnon to Portland, 15 January 1796, C.O. 217, vol. 112, f. 148.

7 Council, 1 August 1798, *ibid.*, vol. 115, ff. 216-218.

8 Diary of a trip to Cape Breton, 17 July 1805, Inglis Papers, M.G. 23, C 6, vol. 6.

9 Despard to Hobart, 2 March 1803, C.O. 217, vol. 121, ff. 45-47.

10 Despard to Windham, 16 February 1807, *ibid.*, vol. 125, ff. 18, 64.

11 Despard to Castlereagh, 26 February 1806, *ibid.*, vol. 124, ff. 26-28.

12 Council, 3 December 1801, *ibid.*, vol 120, f. 27.

13 Despard to Portland, 18 December 1800, *ibid.*, vol. 118, ff. 340-341.

14 Stephen Cottrell to John King, 28 July 1801, *ibid.*, vol. 119, ff, 176-177.

15 Council, 1 August 1802, *ibid.*, vol. 121, f. 8.

16 *Ibid.*

17 Council, 20 July 1803, *ibid.*, vol. 122, f. 33.

18 Earl Camden to Despard, 7 June 1804, *ibid.*, ff. 73-75.

19 Despard to Hobart, 4 March 1803, *ibid.*, vol. 121, ff. 49-50.

20 Council, 21 August 1806, *ibid.*, vol. 125, ff. 11-12.

21 A.C. Dodd, "Observations," 1805 (written in 1816), *ibid.*, vol. 134, f. 148; J.P. Parker, *Cape Breton Ships and Men* (Toronto, 1967) 26.

9. "Cape Breton's Brief Time of Independence Was Over" 1820

1 "A Return showing the Number of Men capable of bearing Arms, The Total Population and Quantity of Stock in the Island of Cape Breton, June 1st, 1813," Cape Breton A 5, pp. 555-573.

2 Ainslie to Bathurst, 25 November 1816, C.O. 217, vol. 134, f. 27.

3 A.A. Johnston, *A History of the Catholic Church in Eastern Nova Scotia* (Antigonish, 1960) vol. 1, p. 277.

4 Reverend Hibbert Binney to the SPG, 4 September 1817, SPG Papers, vol. 31, pp. 299-301.

5 D.C. Harvey, "Scottish Immigration to Cape Breton," *Dalhousie Review*, XXI, 1941-1942, 316.

6 John and Jonathan Tremain to Nepean, 2 September 1811, C.O. 217, vol. 129, f. 64.

7 Ainslie to the Commissioners of His Majesty's Customs, 8 April 1818, Custons and Plantations Papers, vol. 6219, f. 174.

8 Ainslie to Bathurst, 7 July 1818, C.O. 217, vol. 138, ff. 80-81.

9 Ainslie to Goulbourn (private), 15 February 1820, *ibid.*, f. 30.

10 "Petition of the Inhabitants of the North Eastern District of Cape Breton," 7 August 1819, *ibid.*, f. 13.

10. Separatism in Cape Breton 1820-1845

1 *Spirit of the Times*, Sydney, September 1844, Beaton Institute.

2 Kempt to Bathurst, 26 March 1821, London, Public Record Office, Colonial Office (hereafter P.R.O., C.O.) 217, vol. 140. ff. 36-37.

3 Beaton Institute, copy of a petition to George Robert Ainslie, 10 November 1819.

4 Binney to SPG, 3 December 1822, PAC, SPG Papers, Manuscript Group 17, B 1, vol. 34, pp. 12-18.

5 Ainslie to Goulbourn (private), 12 February 1820, P.R.O., C.O. 217, vol. 138, f. 31.

6 Binney to SPG, 12 January 1821, PAC, vol. 33, pp. 94-97.

7 Kempt to Marshall, 16 December 1823, PANS, M.G. 1, vol. 1283/430.

8 Falkland to Stanley, 2 December 1844, P.R.O., C.O. 217, vol. 195, ff. 70-71.

9 Richard Brown, *A History of the Island of Cape Breton* (London: Sampson Low, 1869) p. 447.

10 *Cape Breton Advocate*, Sydney, 18 November 1840.

11 *Ibid.*

12 Kempt to Bathurst, 19 October 1821, P.R.O., C.O. 217, vol. 140, f. 89.

13 There were only two polls in Cape Breton: one at Sydney, the other at Arichat. The results were:

	Sydney	Arichat
Dodd	210	17
Gibbons	139	1
Kavanagh	42	288
Uniacke	42	288

[14] D.C. Douglas, *English Historical Documents*, vol. IV (Eyre and Spotteswoode, 1914) p. 640.

[15] Beaton Institute, Petition, 1833, pp. 14-16.

[16] Douglas, *English Historical Documents*, p. 640.

[17] Royal Instructions to Governor Parr, 11 September 1784, B.I.N.S., vol. 40, p. 123, PANS.

[18] *Ibid.*, p. 123.

[19] For a fuller consideration of this case, see R.J. Morgan, *Orphan Outpost: Cape Breton Colony 1784-1820* (Ph.D. thesis, University of Ottawa, 1972).

[20] The case is clearly stated in a petition directed to the Colonial Office in 1843, C.O. 217, vol. 195, ff. 79-89.

[21] George R. Young, *Letters To The Right Honourable Lord Stanley, H.M. Secretary of State for the Colonies* (Halifax: R. Nugent), PANS.

[22] Brown, *A History of the Island*, pp. 446-447; Great Britain, *Parliamentary Debates*, 1823, vol. VIII, 684-691.

[23] H. Brougham to R. Gibbons, "Opinion," 12 May 1823, Beaton Institute, M.G. 1, D 24.

[24] Petition, 1819, f. 73; "Petition of the Inhabitants of the North Eastern District of Cape Breton," 7 August 1819, C.O. 217, vol. 137, f. 73.

[25] Victoria County was not constituted until 1851.

[26] G.R. Young, *Letters to the Right Honourable Lord Stanley*, p. 14.

[27] A.B. MacEachern to Rev. Aeneas MacDonald, 14 November 1823, M.G. 24, vol. 137, f. 73.

[28] *Cape Breton Advocate*, Sydney, 20 January, 3 February, 1841; G.R. Young, *Letters to the Right Honourable Lord Stanley*, p. 1.

[29] *Ibid.*

[30] Beaton Institute, "Petition of the Inhabitants of Cape Breton against the Annexation of Cape Breton to Nova Scotia...," 1833.

[31] Beaton Institute, M.G.1, E 2. The petition for 1836 is referred to in the 1838 petition to Lord Durham.

[32] The members of the committee were Edmund Murray Dodd, MLA, William R. Bown, Thomas Bown, merchants, Charles R. Ward and William Ouseley, retired major.

[33] J.S. Martin (private secretary of Lord Aberdeen) to A. MacKenzie (counsel for the petitioner), 28 March 1835, Beaton Institute, M.G. 1, E 21.

[34] PAC, M.G. 9, B 4, "Petition of Charles Ward, Chairman and People of Cape Breton Against Annexation, to Lord Durham," 20 June 1838.

[35] C.P. Lucas, ed. *Lord Durham's Report On The Affairs of British North America*, vol. II (Oxford: Clarendon, 1912) pp. 320-322.

[36] *Cape Breton Advocate*, Sydney, 4 November 1840.

[37] *Ibid.*, 3 February 1841.

38 Beaton Institute, "Petitions," 1833, p. 34.

39 *Cape Breton Advocate*, Sydney, 6 October 1840, extract of a letter from Arichat.

40 *Ibid.*, 3 February, 10 February 1841.

41 G.R. Young, *Letters to the Right Honourable Lord Stanley*, p. 13.

42 *Ibid.*, p. 14.

43 *Cape Breton Advocate*, Sydney, 4 November 1840.

44 *Ibid.*, 17 March 1840.

45 Henry Bliss to Lord Stanley, 16 January 1843, C.O. 217, vol. 195, ff. 75-76; Lord Wharnscliffe to Stanley, 3 July 1843, *ibid.*, ff. 137-138; G.W. Hope to Stanley, 27 June 1843, *ibid.*, ff. 142-145.

46 G. Maule to unknown (1843), C.O. 217, vol. 195, ff. 9-10; note on Bliss to Stanley, 16 January 1843, *ibid.*, vol. 195, ff. 75-76; draft letter (Stanley) to Bliss, 25 January 1843, *ibid.*, C.O. 217, vol. 195, f. 77.

47 Note in W. Hope to Bliss, 21 November 1843, *ibid.*

48 Stanley to Goulbourn, 30 March 1844, Goulbourn Papers, accession 319, 11/23, Surrey Record Office, England; *ibid.*, 8 May 1844.

49 Falkland to Stanley (private and confidential), 2 December 1844, C.O. 217, vol. 195, ff. 68-71.

50 Stanley to Falkland, 3 June 1844, *ibid.*, F. 5.

51 Address of the Legislative Assembly to Lord Aberdeen, 27 July 1844, *ibid.*, ff. 15-19.

52 *Ibid.*, 3 June 1844, f. 8.

53 John MacDonnell, *Reports on State Trials*, New Series, Vol. VI (London: Biddles, 1970) Column (hereafter Col.) 393.

54 *Ibid.*, Col. 296.

55 *Ibid.*, Col. 299.

56 *Ibid.*, Col. 300.

57 Bliss to Grey, 8 October 1846, C.O. 217, vol. 195, ff. 122-129. Richard Brown who wrote *Cape Breton* in 1869 could remember the case and claimed (p. 451) that the decision was considered unconstitutional by several "eminent lawyers" of that day.

58 Bliss to Grey, 8 October 1846, C.O. 217, vol. 195, f. 129.

12. "Poverty, wretchedness, and misery": The Great Famine in Cape Breton 1845-1851

1 Agriculture Canada, *Diseases and Pests of Potatoes* (Ottawa, 1973) pp. 8-9.

2 Grant MacEwan, *Harvest of Bread* (Saskatoon, 1969) p. 132.

3 Thomas Leaver (Antigonish) to Caroline Leaver (Baddeck), 19 April 1843, Leaver Papers, M.G. 12/70, letter 16, Beaton Institute.

4 *Journals of the Proceedings of the Nova Scotia House of Assembly* (hereafter *Journals*) 1846, Appendix 77, pp. 240-241.

5 RG 5, Series GP, vol. 4, petition 32, 1 May 1845, PANS.

6 *Journals*, 1846, Appendix 77, pp. 235, 238-9, 258-9, 386, 388, 414, 415; *The Spirit of the Times* (Sydney) 28 January 1846.

7 *Novascotian* (Halifax) 11 December 1833.

8   RG 5, Series P, vol. 83, petition 109, 30 December 1845; petition 67, 25 January 1847, PANS.

9   James Hunter, *The Making of the Crofting Community* (Edinburgh, 1978) pp. 34-39; Douglas Campbell and Raymond MacLean, *Beyond the Atlantic Roar: A Study of the Nova Scotia Scots* (Toronto, 1974) pp. 16-18.

10   *Ibid.*, p. 22.

11   Abraham Gesner, *The Industrial Resources of Nova Scotia* (Halifax, 1849) p. 72.

12   J.S. Martell, *Immigration to and Emigration from Nova Scotia 1815-1838* (Halifax, 1942) p. 10.

13   Charles W. Dunn, *Highland Settler* (Toronto, 1953; rep. Wreck Cove, NS: Breton Books, 1991), pp. 28-29.

14   *Novascotian*, 1 August 1832; 30 October 1833; 11 December 1833; 9 April 1834.

15   Data is a summary of following sources: *Novascotian*, 15 September 1845; *Journals*, 1846, Appendix 77, pp. 240-241; *ibid.*, 1847, Appendix 70, p. 277; *ibid.*, Appendix 39, pp. 189, 193, 195, 197; *ibid.*, 1848, Appendix 39, pp. 154-5; *ibid.*, 1849, Appendix 100, pp. 578-584; *ibid.*, 1850, Appendix 45, pp. 163-171; *ibid.*, 1851, Appendix 42, p. 172; *Cape Breton News* (Sydney) 24 November 1852; J.S. Martell, *From Central Board to Secretary of Agriculture, 1826-1885* (Halifax, 1940) pp. 7-11.

16   RG 5, Series P, vol. 83, petition 176, 14 December 1847, PANS.

17   *Journals*, 1846, Appendix 77, p. 238.

18   RG 5, Series P, vol. 83, petition 138, 3 May 1847; petition 144, 29 May 1847, PANS.

19   *Novascotian*, 7 June 1847.

20   *The Times and Cape Breton Spectator* (Sydney), 17 March 1849; *Novascotian*, 9 April 1849.

21   RG 5, Series P, vol. 83, petition 135, 21 April 1847, PANS; *Cape Breton Spectator*, 6 May 1848.

22   *Journals*, 1847, Appendix 70, p. 195.

23   *Novascotian*, 1 May 1848.

24   *The Times and Cape Breton Spectator*, 17 March 1849.

25   RG 5, Series P, vol. 83, petition 135, 21 April 1847, PANS.

26   "Katy Mary," unpublished manuscript, Florence R. MacLeod Papers; M.G. 12/194, Beaton Institute. Mr. Bremner probably refers to Arthur Brymer (1777-1847), MLA for Richmond County, 1846-47.

27   RG 5, Series P, vol. 83, petition 144, 20 May 1847, PANS.

28   Norman McLeod to John Gordon, 1 June 1848, in *Letters of the Reverend Norman McLeod 1835-1851*, D.C. Harvey ed. *Bulletin of the Public Archives of Nova Scotia*, II (1), 1939, p. 22.

29   *Novascotian*, 1 December 1845; 18 October 1847.

30   *Journals*, 1847, Appendix 39, p. 197.

31   Gesner, *Industrial Resources* (Halifax, 1849) p. 200.

32   RG 5, Series P, vol. 53, petition 85, 26 February 1847, PANS; M.G. 1, vol. 711, No. 27, PANS; copied from *Presbyterian Witness* (Halifax), 14 September

1850.

33 *Presbyterian Witness*, 15 August 1851.

34 RG 5, Series P, vol. 84, petition 68, 1848, PANS.

35 *Ibid.*, petition 55, 29 February 1848.

36 RG 5, Series GP, vol. 7, petition 35, 1 May 1845; vol. 9, petition 8, 1848, PANS.

37 RG 5, Series P, vol. 53, No. 74, 27 January 1847, PANS.

38 *Journals*, 1846, p. 388; *Novascotian*, 19 January 1846.

39 *Journals*, 1847, Appendix 73, pp. 280-281.

40 RG 5, Series P, vol. 83, petition 106, 10 February 1847; petition 138, 3 May 1847, PANS.

41 N. McLeod to John Gordon, 22 August 1848, in Harvey, *Letters*, p. 23.

42 *Cape Breton Spectator*, 6 May 1848.

43 RG 5, Series P, vol. 83, petition 109, 30 December 1846; vol. 84, petition 24, 5 February 1848, PANS.

44 *Journals*, 1848, Appendix 67.

45 Norman McLeod to John Gordon, 1 June 1848, in Harvey, *Letters*, p. 21; RG 5, Series P, vol. 84, petition 24, 5 February 1848, PANS.

46 *Novascotian*, 1 May 1848.

47 *Journals*, 1848, Appendix 67.

48 *Novascotian*, 1 May 1848.

49 *Novascotian*. 1 May 1848; *Journals*, 1848, Appendix 67.

50 *Journals*, 1848, Appendix 67.

51 *Novascotian*, 1 May 1848.

52 *Novascotian*, 26 January 1846.

53 *Novascotian*, 30 November 1846.

54 *Presbyterian Witness*, 16 July 1853.

55 *Cape Breton Advocate*, 13 May 1848.

56 Campbell, *Atlantic Roar*, p. 73.

57 D. MacDonald, *Cape North and Vicinity* (Port Hastings, 1933) p. 21.

58 John L. MacDougall, *History of Inverness County* (Port Hastings, 1922) p. 91.

59 William McKeen Papers, M.G. 12/109, documents 1424-1435, 1377(a), Beaton Institute.

60 This could help to account for the increasing use of English in nineteenth-century Cape Breton. One researcher has found that people failed to teach their children Gaelic in later years because "they felt English was more useful." Amy L. Varen, "Two Linguistic Revival Movements: Gaelic in Cape Breton Island, Nova Scotia, and in Brittany" (unpublished B.A. thesis, Harvard, 1975) p. 8.

61 *Cape Breton Advocate*, 9 September 1840.

62 Abraham Gesner, *Industrial Resources*, p. 12; M.L. Hansen, *The Mingling of the Canadian and American Peoples* (New Haven, 1939), p. 122; Mrs. R.G. Flewelling, "Immigration to and Emigration from Nova Scotia 1839-1851," in *Collections* of the Nova Scotia Historical Society, XXVIII (1949) 104.

63 Rev. Michael Brosnan, *Pioneer History of the Parish of St. George's, Newfoundland* (Toronto, 1848) p. 13, cited in Margaret B. Knight, "Some Aspects

12/04

of the Scottish Gaelic Traditions of the Codroy Valley, Newfoundland" (unpublished M.A. thesis, Memorial University, 1975) p. 58; Rosemary Ommer, "Scots Kinship, Migration and Early Settlement in South East Newfoundland" (unpublished M.A. thesis, Memorial University, 1973) pp. 16, 28, 65.

64 Flewelling, *Immigration and Emigration*, p. 104. For a full account of Norman McLeod's career in Cape Breton, see Laurie Stanley, *The Well-Watered Garden* (Sydney: University College of Cape Breton Press, 1983), and Flora McPherson, *Watchman Against the World* (London, 1962; rep. Wreck Cove, NS: Breton Books, 1993).

65 Norman McLeod to John Gordon, 1 June 1848, in Harvey, *Letters*, p. 22.

66 RG 5, Series GP, Vol. 6, petition 24, 6 February 1849, PANS.

67 Stanley, *The Well-Watered Garden*, p. 168; Harvey, *Letters*, p. 26.

68 *Novascotian*, 9 September 1850.

69 *Ibid.*

70 Flewelling, *Immigration and Emigration*, pp. 85-85; *Novascotian*, 2 October 1841.

71 Michael Flinn et al., *Scottish Population History* (Cambridge, 1977) p. 446.

72 *Ibid.*, pp. 421-438.

73 *Ibid.*, p. 438.

74 *Ibid.*, pp. 466-467.

75 Sir John Harvey to Earl Grey, 1 April 1847, in *Journals*, 1848, pp. 42-43.

76 Grey to Harvey, 29 April 1847, *ibid*, pp. 42, 44.

77 Flewelling, *Immigration and Emigration*, p. 94; Campbell, *Atlantic Roar*, p. 23.

78 Flewelling, *Immigration and Emigration*, p. 87.

79 *Journals*, 1847, Appendix 70, pp. 208-209.

80 *Ibid.*

81 *Ibid.*, p. 277.

82 RG 5, Series P, vol. 53, petition 74, 27 January 1847, PANS.

83 *Journals*, 1848, Appendix 86.

84 *Journals*, 1849, Appendix 100, pp. 578-9, 584.

85 *Ibid.*, 1850, Appendix 45, p. 171.

86 *Novascotian*, 28 October 1850; *Journals*, 1851, Appendix 42, p. 172.

87 Martell, *Immigration and Emigration*, pp. 10-11.

88 Gesner, *Industrial Resources*, p. 200.

89 *Cape Breton News*, 24 November 1852.

90 *Ibid.*, 20 October 1852.